George William Manby

Journal of a Voyage to Greenland

1821

George William Manby

Journal of a Voyage to Greenland

1821

ISBN/EAN: 9783954272259
Erscheinungsjahr: 2012
Erscheinungsort: Bremen, Deutschland

© maritimepress in Europäischer Hochschulverlag GmbH & Co. KG, Fahrenheitstr. 1, 28359 Bremen. Alle Rechte beim Verlag und bei den jeweiligen Lizenzgebern.

www.maritimepress.de | office@maritimepress.de

Bei diesem Titel handelt es sich um den Nachdruck eines historischen, lange vergriffenen Buches. Da elektronische Druckvorlagen für diese Titel nicht existieren, musste auf alte Vorlagen zurückgegriffen werden. Hieraus zwangsläufig resultierende Qualitätsverluste bitten wir zu entschuldigen.

JOURNAL

OF A

VOYAGE TO GREENLAND,

IN THE YEAR 1821.

WITH GRAPHIC ILLUSTRATIONS.

BY GEORGE WILLIAM MANBY, Esq.

THE SECOND EDITION.

LONDON:
PRINTED FOR G. AND W. B. WHITTAKER,
AVE-MARIA LANE.

MDCCCXXIII.

TO THE RIGHT HONOURABLE

SIR BENJAMIN BLOOMFIELD,

&c. &c. &c.

My dear Sir,

In availing myself of the permission, so kindly given, to dedicate to you this Volume, it were an equal want of good feeling as of good taste, to repeat those praises which the general voice of the nation has long pronounced upon your public character; but I may be allowed to state, with conscious pride, that in early life, when Cadets at the Royal Military Academy, Woolwich, you were my guide, my leader, and my friend; and it is a great pleasure to me to know that you also can look back with pleasure to our intimacy in those times,

" memor
" Actæ non alio rege puertiæ,
" Mutatæque simul togæ."

I have the honour to be,

With the profoundest respect,

Your devoted and humble Servant,

GEORGE W. MANBY.

Barracks at Yarmouth,
July 19, 1822.

INTRODUCTION.

My views were originally directed to the undertaking which forms the subject of the present Volume, by a suggestion of the late Right Honourable George Rose, when President of the Board of Trade. On witnessing some experiments made by me to illustrate my method of saving persons from shipwreck, he was pleased to declare his conviction that the principle there employed, in the projection of a rope from a gun, might be extended with much advantage to the whale-fishery, for the purpose of throwing a harpoon in a similar manner. He expressed his own confidence that the general introduction of such a change, would, in a great degree, avert the failure, which he regretted to learn, had latterly attended the investment of capital in this branch of commercial speculation; and he at the same time inquired my opinion, how far that failure was generally susceptible of remedy, either by improvement in the present method of taking whales, or by such alterations in the construction of the implements used in the business, as should tend to give greater security to those engaged in the enterprise. After remarking that the Greenland whale-fishery afforded the best nursery for a hardy race of sailors, that, if successful, it would give employment to much shipping and numerous artificers, and was calculated to produce valuable cargoes for the comfort and convenience of life, without sending money out of the country, he concluded by a flattering wish that I should apply my attention to this subject of paramount national importance.

It was a sufficient motive for exertion, that my efforts were encouraged by the favourable expectations of this distinguished individual who had so eloquently and successfully advocated my plan for rescue from shipwreck. If, however, a further incentive to indefatigable perseverance had been requisite, I should have found it in the zealous desire to shew gratitude to my country for that generous patronage, which had enabled me to carry into execution my invention for protecting her seamen from the horrors of a watery grave. I shall be pardoned if I here remark, with some degree of pride and satisfaction, that this invention, has already been crowned with success in the preservation of ONE HUNDRED AND FIFTY-SIX PERSONS, as well foreigners as natives, saved within my own immediate knowledge, who, under Heaven, are indebted for their lives to the philanthropy of the British Government.

It was under the influence of these feelings, that I became a painful observer of the consequences entailed upon the port of Yarmouth by the general stagnation of trade and commercial difficulty, which unhappily visited this empire for years after the return of peace. The effects of this total suspension of mercantile activity were distressingly visible in the forest of dismantled shipping, that crowded the harbour of Yarmouth, and in the wretched appearance of the numerous seamen, who were discarded to wander over the country in the vain search after employment and livelihood. In no way, I considered, could my exertions be so availing, or so beneficially applied, as in the endeavour to promote a revival of that valuable speculation in the whale-fishery, which had for years been laid aside at this port. I confidently indulged in the hope that if I could ensure success where it had hitherto been doubtful, adventure might again be encouraged; first, to the attainment of a local advantage for Yarmouth, and, subsequently, to the production of a common national benefit.

After perfecting my designs, proving their utility by experiment, and obtaining the favourable opinion of several men of eminence in the scientific world, I entered into an extensive correspondence, upon the state of the whale-fishery, with individuals of well known experience in that line. My purpose was particularly to ascertain their sentiments relative to the gun-harpoon, to learn why that implement was not in more general use, and to inquire into the causes of the prejudice which existed in various quarters against its adoption. But I found it impossible to collect from their statements any satisfactory reason for the rejection of an instrument which had been strenuously patronised by the Society of Arts, Commerce, and Manufactures, and the excellence of which was self-evident. I could not resist the conjecture that the neglect of it must proceed from some cause, the knowledge of which was withheld from the proprietors in the concern, and I was convinced that they were sustaining great injury from the ignorance or prejudices of their subordinate agents.

To ascertain a fact involving no less a consideration than the annual saving of immense sums to the nation, with the employment of many ships, seamen, and artificers, could only, I found, be successfully attempted by a voyage in a whale ship, and I resolved to undertake the expedition accordingly. I was fortunate in finding an opportunity of sailing with Captain Scoresby, who was proceeding from Liverpool in command of the Greenland ship, the Baffin. The merits of Captain Scoresby, as an arctic navigator, are too generally acknowledged to need the aid of my testimony to his skill and intrepidity; and I regarded it with reason as no trifling advantage in the projected voyage, that my observation would be assisted by the fruits of his talents and experience.

Such were the circumstances under which I performed the voyage to Greenland, detailed in the following pages. In submitting my narrative to the indulgence of the public, I have studiously endeavoured to offer a plain and faithful statement of every occurrence of moment which fell under my notice. Considerations will thus be suggested for removing the obstacles and for diminishing the dangers which have so frequently led to failure in the whale-fishery; and I trust that if, from inability to obtain fair experiment, the principal object of my undertaking was deprived of success, it will at least be found that my voyage has neither been altogether devoid of utility to the nation, nor of interest to the general reader.

VOYAGE

TO

GREENLAND.

April 6, 1821. AT twelve o'clock, the Baffin went out of the Queen's Dock at Liverpool. This circumstance drew together an immense concourse of people, not excited only by the interest attached to the expedition which the ship was about to undertake, but by the high nautical reputation and amiable character of her commander. The affectionate farewells of several of the spectators to their friends on board, proved that warmer feelings than the curiosity of the crowd had drawn *them* to the spot. As soon as we had cleared the basin, three hearty cheers from the by-standers greeted us, to speak their best wishes for our success and safe return, and our ship's company returned the sincere acknowledgment of their thanks in a similar manner. The wind being a-head, we warped to a buoy at some distance from the shore, and loosened the sails; on the tide swinging the ship round, we unmoored and stood to the south-west; and when, by sailing in on the other tack, we came opposite the quay where the ship was built, three cheers from the carpenters again bespoke a solicitude for our welfare, and as usual were replied to: at three o'clock, we reached the new deep off Blackrock, where, from the state of the wind, finding it impossible to proceed to sea, we let go our anchor. Some friends of our captain, and the owners of the ship, having accompanied us thus far, dined on board. Shortly after the party left us, I retired to my cabin, where, in the night, I felt the inconvenience of a tight ship; for the wind blowing hard, agitated the bilge water and oleaginous matter left last voyage, to the production of a gas of so extremely pungent a nature, as to render respiration difficult, and almost to produce suffocation; and so great was its influence upon all metallic substances in the vessel, that it turned them completely black.

April 8. The morning dawned beautifully clear; and soon after breakfast, one of the owners came on board with three clerical gentlemen; and preparations were made between decks for service, which was attended by the whole crew, whose devotion and religious deportment, qualities so rarely seen in populous places of public worship, did honour to their Christian feelings. Captain Scoresby read the prayers and lessons for the day, in a most impressive manner; and on his concluding, one of the clergymen offered up a fervent supplication to Almighty God, to extend his blessings and protection in all cases of difficulty and danger to which his congregation would soon be exposed; another then delivered an appropriate lecture to the crew, on the duty and advantage of reliance on God's goodness in distress, and other visitations of Providence. At three o'clock, just on the first of the ebb tide, we weighed anchor, and the wind being light, put two boats a-head, and sailed towards the floating light, where our pilot left us. At eight o'clock, the captain, as I found to be his usual custom in concluding the Sabbath, ordered all the boys and young men into his cabin, alternately to read a verse in the Bible, for three or four chapters: after this, we all fell upon our knees, and he offered up an extempore and most impressive prayer, which, for composition and fervent supplication, I have seldom heard excelled, and which I shall, with his permission, here annex.

A PRAYER ON THE COMMENCEMENT OF A VOYAGE TO GREENLAND.

Almighty God, the King immortal, invisible, eternal, who art the creator and preserver of mankind, in knowledge of whom standeth our eternal life, and whose service is perfect freedom, we would approach thy footstool with the voice of supplication and prayer, and with thanksgivings would make known our requests unto thee.

Though we, from our numerous iniquities, are not worthy to come into thy divine presence, nor can be entitled to the least ac of thy favour; though our best actions in the view of infinite purity must be unclean, and insufficient to answer unto thee for a single sin, yet, we bless thee, that, through the merits of our Saviour, we are encouraged to come humbly to thy throne, that we may obtain mercy, and find grace to help us in every time of need. We esteem it our privilege, as well as our duty, to bow the knee before thee, and rejoice in the opportunity of seeking thy blessing on the adventurous voyage on which we are now embarked. Go out with us on the expanse of the ocean; be with us when the raging elements proclaim the power of divinity; and direct us, merciful God, with thy heavenly wisdom. Uphold us with thine almighty care; further us with thy continual help; prosper us with success and happiness; restore us in thine own good time to those, who, by the ties of kindred, or the bonds of affection, are near and dear to us; and, finally after this life, bring us and them to thine everlasting kingdom, through Jesus Christ our Lord. Thou, O God, hast hitherto manifested thyself unto us as a prayer-hearing, and a prayer-answering God; thou hast heard our petitions in the midst of danger; hast delivered us from numerous perils; and hast directed and supported us in many difficulties. Thou hast been, and still art, a present help in every time of need. Grant us, we beseech thee, a continuance of thy favour; preserve us while we trace the treacherous deep, from every evil; from rocks and shoals; from fire and tempest; from sea and ice; from distress and accident; and from every danger, seen and unseen, known and unknown. Sanctify the dispensations of thy providence to usward, whether prosperous or adverse, agreeable or painful. And evermore give us such reliance on thy faithfulness, and such dependance on the excellence of thy government, that we may fully commit our ways unto thee, for thou wilt sustain us. To this end, O heavenly Father, may we be endowed with the sacred influence of thy Holy Spirit; may we read thy word with profit, and find it to be the power of God unto salvation; may we be earnest and constant in prayer; may we be delivered from sin, and not from its condemning influence alone, but also from its hardening and ruling power; may we cultivate a spiritual frame of mind by the diligent use of every means of grace, and by avoiding whatever may grieve the Holy Spirit; and may we manfully resist the lusts of the flesh that war against the soul; the lusts of the eye, the pride of life, and all other besetting sin. Then shall we experience the blessing of religion, and prove that her ways are ways of pleasantness, and that all her paths are peace.

Bless now, O Lord, all for whom it is our duty to pray—our wives, our children, our parents, our kindred, our friends: may they have favour at the hands of the Lord, and be made partakers of the salvation of Jesus: though separated by an expanse of waters, we may yet meet in heart at the throne of grace. Preserve them, we beseech thee, in our absence; be unto them a husband, a father, a friend; and, if it please thee in thine infinite mercy, to restore us to each other, may we again unite in adoration to thee for thy protecting goodness.

Bless the sailors, our companions in this voyage of anxiety and peril; may they be obedient to the will of God: and when they behold thy wonders in the deep, grant them grace to acknowledge thy sovereignty, thy mercy, and thy power.

We thank thee, O Lord, for the mercies with which we are so richly surrounded: while thousands of our fellow-creatures are pining in misery and want, we are permitted bountifully to enjoy every necessary, and almost every luxury, of life; and while many are given up to a hard and wicked heart, to work all mischief with greediness, and to sin against thee with a high hand; we praise thee that thou hast restrained us from gross iniquity, and especially if thou hast given us the power of religion in our hearts.

We now commend ourselves to thy fatherly care and protection: keep us, we beseech thee, from evil, and lead us into the knowledge of salvation through Jesus Christ. Pardon our manifold iniquities, and grant us a blessing according to thy promise, that when two or three are gathered together in thy name, then wilt thou be in the midst: fulfil, O Lord, every desire and petition as far as thou shalt see good for us, giving us in this world knowledge of thy truth, and in the world to come, life everlasting. These, with all other mercies, needful or good for us, as well for the body as the soul, we ask in the prevailing name of Jesus Christ; to whom, with the Father and the Holy Ghost, be endless praises. Amen.

On passing the south end of the Isle of Man, where two light-houses are placed, to warn the incautious navigator of his proximity to the dangerous rocks, called " the Chickens," we altered our course for what is termed the north-about passage, or north-channel, thereby keeping the Scottish coast to the eastward, and Ireland to the westward. Occasional indistinct glimpses of both coasts were seen; but, on account of the haziness of the atmosphere, no particular spot could be recognised. The ship's company were mustered and divided into watches, and persons were appointed to the boats. To the service of the boat intended to carry my harpoon-gun, as follows: Richard Simpkin, harpooner; Thomas Serjeant, boat-steerer; a line-coiler; and four others to the oars. No sooner had we cleared the coasts of Ireland and Scotland, than the heavy Atlantic swell met us. Then! oh, then! came the long-dreaded and much-expected malady of sea-sickness; and continued, with very little intermission, for nearly a fortnight: during which time, I took scarcely any nourishment; so that, with an emaciated frame, and unshorn beard, I became as pitiable an object as the sun ever beheld. Unusual as it is to meet with sympathy under sea-sickness, which, on the contrary, is rather a source of merriment to all but the sufferer, I really believe, that when I was capable of reaching the deck, the commiseration of every one on board was sincerely given to me. I endeavoured to resign myself to the evils of the disorder, my only dread being, lest I should not be able to accomplish what was so much the object of my voyage—the making improvements in the whale-fishery. Feeling, as I do, for the sufferings of others by violent sea-sickness, sufferings beyond the power of language to describe, I exhort medical men to pay attention to the malady, either to its prevention, or to the mitigation of its effects: they would thus confer a blessing on many, and would receive that best and most grateful reward—a self-approving heart, in having afforded comfort to their fellow-creatures under a most distressing and overpowering disease.

April 16. During one of the short intervals in the abatement of the malady, in which I was able to reach the deck, we passed close on the westward side of the Ferroe Islands. They were much obscured by mist: but at intervals, the sun had power to dispel it, and they presented themselves, many in number, and of varied extent, shewing perpendicular cliffs, and other rugged features, with glens much furrowed by the torrents of rain. Of those violent winds, for which they are so renowned, we experienced a specimen in such gusts, as threatened to rend the sails from the yards of the ship. The coast that we saw was without vegetation or fertilized soil, without sign of habitation and apparently destined to be a residence rather for birds than for man. These islands are subject to the dominion of Denmark; they are twenty-five in number, extending from latitude 61° 15' to 62° 10 north. When the day is at the greatest length in them, the sun rises at seven minutes past two, and sets at fifty-three minutes past nine o'clock; on the shortest day, the sun rises at fifty-three minutes past nine, and sets at seven minutes past two. These islands were discovered and peopled in the reign of Harold Haarfager, king of Norway, and Griener Camban was the first inhabitant of one of them. The Christian religion being fully established in Denmark, about the year 1000, the Gospel was propagated, a bishop appointed to these islands, and Stromoe fixed as his place of residence; the diocese consists of seven parishes and thirty-nine churches. The islands are, together with Iceland, under one governor; but different subordinate officers superintend the trade carried on between them and Copenhagen.

In passing the latitude in which Iceland lies, I observed several Solan geese, *(Pelicanus Bassanus,* LINN.,) singly passing, and each pursuing the same direct course, from that island to the Ferroes. The setting of the sun this evening, was attended with the richest tinted clouds I had ever beheld, and when the great luminary had sunken below the surface of the deep, it left its reflected representation, (though of an oblong form,) for a considerable time hanging in the curtain of heaven.

April 19. The wind, which had hitherto been favourable, changed to north-east; blew strong with snow, and increased with a degree of violence, that caused the sea to rage to a greater height than I had ever before witnessed: part of the bulwark was stove in; and, by a stroke on the rudder, a man was projected over the wheel, and nearly overboard.

April 21. The gale beginning to subside, I felt better; struggled to rally, and by the fineness of the day, was encouraged to go upon deck; but was reduced to such a state of weakness and debility, that I was unable to walk without the aid of Captain Scoresby's arm. As Saturday was generally closed with mirth by the crew, I took the opportunity of conforming to the custom expected of every one on his first voyage to Greenland, that is, to pay what is termed the "cape bottle;" I therefore sent two pounds of sugar, half a pound of coffee, and one pound of tobacco, to each mess, as my tribute. It began to blow hard in the evening, and the following day, Easter-Sunday, the storm grew so violent, and the severity of temperature was so much beyond any thing to which I had hitherto been accustomed, (the thermometer being ten degrees below the freezing point) that I became quite unable to keep the deck.

April 23. This day we crossed the Arctic or northern polar circle in 6° 28', west longitude, about noon, the wind blowing hard.

April 25. The swell occasioned by the gale having subsided, harpoons were delivered to the harpooners to be cleaned, sharpened, and the foreganger, or rope immediately attached to the harpoon, to be spanned on the socket at the shank of the weapon. I was much amused with this last process, as there were interwoven in the rope, at distances of two or three feet, pieces of riband of various colours. These decorations I was informed were the gifts of the men's sweethearts; on some, I observed pieces that had undergone the useful office of garters; this at once elucidated the " magic spell," as they were intended to animate the powers of the harpooner, who derives fame, and consequently, the approbation of his lass, in proportion to the number of whales he is able to strike and to capture.

April 29. I had a most refreshing night's rest; and the brightness of the sun, reflecting through the convex lens into my cabin, urged me to rise early: a more beautiful day never shone from the heavens, and I felt infinitely cheered by the influence of the solar rays. Scarcely had my eye met the "vasty deep," all dressed in coldest blue, when it was attracted by pieces of ice, of perfect alabaster whiteness, with which the great circle of ocean was studded. As we proceeded, they increased in size, exciting my admiration and surprise, as I had never seen any thing of the kind before: they resembled human busts, towers, slender spires, massy pyramids, and every other form that it is possible to imagine: varying in height from four to ten feet, and in extent from ten to fifty yards. The rays of the brilliant sun on some of the angles, or sides, which presented inclined planes, reflected a glare of light, that perfectly dazzled my eyes, and which I can only compare to that obtained by the chemical process of inflaming carbon or phosphorus in oxygen. My renovated health gave me this day an opportunity of attending the duties usual in this ship on the Sabbath: morning, afternoon, and evening service, were performed in the most devout manner by our excellent commander, who, in sermons well suited to a sailor's mind, called the attention of his crew to the serious consideration of their past, present, and future lives. In the evening, the wind began to blow strong; and being accompanied with snow, we did not see the sun take its last departure that we were likely to witness for some months; for, if we continued sailing for twenty-four hours longer, in this direction, it would then be our constant companion, and yield us continued day. I remained on the deck this evening till half past ten o'clock, enjoying the benefit of the light. Latitude by observation, 73° north; thermometer 30°.

April 30. Altering our course in the night to the eastward, to get clear of several large masses of ice, much sail was carried on the ship, and having run far enough for that purpose, we changed to our destined course of north-east. Towards the evening the water lost its former blueness, and became less transparent: as we proceeded, it was yet more turbid, and acquired the appearance of dark water, in which whales are said to delight, the surface assuming a dark bottle-green-colour blended with a light brown or brassy tint. These colours are produced, (as discovered by Captain Scoresby) by myriads of small animalculæ of the *Mollusca* family, with which this part of the ocean abounds, and which are so minute, as scarcely to be visible to the eye, even with microscopic aid, several hundreds of them being contained in every drop. These smaller give nourishment to a larger class of medusa, from which whales are supposed to derive a considerable part of their subsistence, filtering or separating them from the fluid by means of two rows of fringed whalebone, which will be spoken of hereafter. Being now in a situation where whales might be seen, and the afternoon being fine, all the crew were called to get up the whale-boats and prepare them for service. These boats are from twenty-five to twenty-seven feet in length, and five and a half in breadth; sharp at both ends, and rather finer at the stern than at the stem. The required properties of these boats are, buoyancy with liveliness in a sea, speed for pursuit, and facility of turning to follow the rapid movements of the whale. The first two of these properties are produced by the rise in the floor, given in their construction; the second, by the fine entrance, and run at each end; and the last by the curvature of the keel. Six lines, of two inches and a quarter in circumference and of one hundred and twenty fathoms in length each, making an extent of one thousand four hundred and forty yards, were distributed to each boat. They were ingeniously coiled in a crate, four feet by one foot eight inches, termed the fore-beck, formed in the middle of the boat, and in another compartment, termed the after-beck, suited to the form of the boat at the stern. Each boat's crew displayed great emulation in preparing their vessels; and on finishing the tedious work, gave three cheers, in the exultation of their hopes. The foreganger of the harpoon being affixed to the line, the harpoon was placed in due form, the head lying upon the bollard (or upright post) let into the boat's bow, and the shaft resting upon a spline with loops in it, called a mik, let into the gunwale. Four lances to despatch a captured fish, a small axe to cut away the line, in case of its getting foul when running out; a wooden fid to splice with, a tail-knife to cut a hole through the tail of the fish, for the convenience of towing it, a small triangular flag, (termed a jack,) on a staff, to hoist in a boat fast to a fish, and six oars, fitted with grummets and tholes with muffles, constituted the equipment of each boat. These boats were then distributed, one over the stern, one over each quarter, one over each of the main chains, and two on the deck, ready to be hoisted out the moment they should be required. The beauty of the evening tempted me not to retire to rest, but to witness the ceremonies of a May-day morning, the celebration of which is an old established custom in Greenland-whale-ships. In the evening a Snow-bunting (*Emberiza nivalis*, LINN.,) was seen flying round the ship, and at length settled upon one of the boats; it probably had been blown off the coast of Greenland, as it appeared much fatigued.

May 1. No sooner had eight bells struck to hail the arrival of the festive day, than the most grotesque group of figures imaginable advanced slowly towards a garland, composed of hoops, decorated with ribands, that was already suspended from the mizen stay, by the last married man in the ship. Here, as usual, three cheers were given. The sailor who personated Neptune, and whose authority all must obey, bearing the emblems of fishing in one hand, and a brazen trumpet in the other, was so extravagantly attired, as to excite the most irresistible laughter. He approached towards me, and inquired whence I came, which, with several other interrogatories, was answered to his apparent satisfaction; but I believe his complacency arose from the remembrance of the "cape bottle," with which I had formerly regaled the crew. His marine majesty now issued orders to his constables, each holding a harpoon shaft, to arrest every person who was similarly situated with myself, on a first voyage, and to bring them before him. They were constrained to go and answer his interrogatories, some of which were of the most humorous and ridiculous kind. I will here describe his appearance: his face was covered with a most unsightly mask: a large full-bottomed wig was on his head, and a loose cloak with a border of old blanket, tufted with rope-yarn to represent ermine, was belted round his body; by his side he had an immense rapier. He was accompanied by several attendants, and his consort rested upon his august arm; she exhibited nothing remarkable besides a whitened face, and a large protuberance in front, to denote that little apprehension need be entertained of a failure of succession to his throne, as it might reasonably be expected from her size, that she would bring forth a litter of little Neptunes. His barber was most appositely dressed, in a clean white shirt, neckcloth, and apron, with powdered hair; he held a monstrous razor made of an iron hoop, one edge having teeth to answer the purpose of a saw. Neptune inquired whether his implement for shaving was sharp, which he examined, and approved: the watery god and his attendants then retired between decks into the galley, where he ordered his prisoners to be brought singly before him, to answer interrogatories, and to undergo the process of shaving. Here all requisites were prepared, lather mixed with soot and grease, and the brush commonly used in tarring the vessel. The ship's steward was the first brought to this arbitrary tribunal, having his eyes bound with a handkerchief, and his hands and feet put into the stocks which were ready for the occasion. He was not arraigned upon charges said to be imputed to him, that is, of not paying his " cape bottle;" but I have since understood, that the offence was one which sailors consider most heinous, that of not only shortening their grog, but reducing its strength;

and I must add, he was inveterately hated by the whole crew. The lathering now commenced, and interrogatories were put by Neptune; and when the unlucky fellow opened his mouth to reply, the brush, saturated with the nauseous compound, was thrust into it. This ceremony was continued for some time, until the toothy edge of the razor had removed the lather from his face, which bore evident marks of retribution having been attained; but the steward's sufferings were not at an end, as he afterwards underwent the process of ablution, which was not of the most delicate nature. Such others as were brought before the tribunal of Neptune, not being charged with any particular offence, and having paid their "cape bottle," were passed over without molestation or inconvenience. The shaving being concluded, the procession was marshalled on deck; and marching round, followed by the melodious tones of frying-pans, kettles, and clashing iron pot-lids, they halted in front of the companion, gave three cheers, and sang "God save the King:" grog, as usual, being then given to them, they peaceably retired to their respective duties, and I to my cabin. In the afternoon it began to blow hard, accompanied by a fall of snow: on examining the snow with the assistance of a microscope, the configurations were stelliform and hexagonal, in the most perfect state.

May 2. The gale continued with uninterrupted violence, keeping the sea in perpetual foam, and rolling mountains high: at four P. M.,

HEAVY ICE WITH ICE BLINK.

London, Pub.d by G & W.B.Whittaker, Ave Maria lane.

we met with many pieces of *heavy** drift-ice; and soon after, a streak of light, resembling the dawning of approaching day, but without its redness, was visible in the air just above the horizon. This appearance which is termed an ice-blink, proceeds from an extensive space, or compact aggregation of ice, which occasions the rays of light, that strike its snowy surface, to be reflected into the superincumbent air, where they become visible; hence, when the ice-blink occurs under the most favourable circumstances, it affords to the eye, a beautiful and perfect map of the ice, twenty or thirty miles beyond the limit of direct vision, but more or less distinct, in proportion as the air is clear or hazy. The ice-blink not only shews the figure of the ice, but enables the experienced observer to judge, whether it, as thus pictured, be field or packed ice; if the latter, whether it be compact or open, bay or heavy ice. Field ice affords the most lucid blink, accompanied with a tinge of yellow; that of packed, is more purely white; and of bay ice, greyish. The land, on account of its snowy covering, likewise occasions a blink, which is yellowish, and not much unlike that produced by the field ice. The nearer we approached to the north, the more numerous were the pieces of ice, until the ocean was covered with them. The wind still blowing into the ice, and finding ourselves embayed,

---

* Pieces that are of a great depth in the water, and dangerous for a ship to strike.

we tacked about, and sailed to the southward. About eleven o'clock at night, I was surprised by the hitherto unusual appearance of the sun shining into the cabin windows. To one who, from his earliest remembrance had witnessed the ordinary division of day and night, as it occurs in our climate, this effect was novel and astonishingly interesting.

May 3. By the continuation of the gale, the ship was still kept embayed in a deep bight of ice; but the wind moderating, we sailed to the eastward, until streams of ice again set limits to our further advance; but, on standing to the south-west, they were soon lost. Just as the steward came on deck, to announce that the cabin-supper was ready, I saw at some distance, a whale blowing: it is impossible to express my feelings on the occasion, or to describe the vehemence with which I shouted—a fish! a fish!! The bustle of all the men coming on deck, and of the different crews jumping into their respective boats, ready for the pursuit, was a scene of most animating activity. The *spectioneer's* (first harpooner) boat was destined for the service, and accordingly lowered. The wind began to increase immediately after, and drifting snow came with a severity that made it very painful to the eyes*, and often obscured the sight

---

* From the cutting effects of the snow, I was induced to examine it through a powerful magnifying glass, and found it to be formed of extremely minute pieces of ice, angularly pointed at their ends, and of prismatic form.

of the boat from us. The ship being in a bay, whose boundary was impenetrable ice, with a gale blowing into it, the probable capture of a whale became a consideration of minor importance, in the breast of our prudent and experienced commander, than the hazard to which the ship and boats might be exposed. I must here add a circumstance that now occurred and regulated, in some measure, the determination of relinquishing the pursuit, and to which I respectfully direct the particular notice of every commander of a vessel at sea. Captain Scoresby being constant in his observance of that faithful monitor, the barometer, which will warn the unwary by its depression in approaching storms, saw that it foretold an impending gale; as such, he called the boat in, took in superfluous sails, and got the ship under close-reefed topsails and courses. This act of judgment was among the numerous proofs which I witnessed of his professional attention; as it soon after blew with greater violence than it had hitherto done during our voyage, and continued with, what is very unusual in this frozen region, torrents of rain all night. Thermometer, at noon, 15°.

May 5. The wind having blown hard from the south-east, all the day before, at length changed to the north-west, and again gathered to a storm with a high rolling sea. The gale abating about six, P.M., numerous flocks of small birds called Rotges, (*Alca Alle*, LINN.,) were seen in every direction, flying, swimming, and diving; and by their appearance bespeaking our approach to ice. At half past seven o'clock, a closely connected *stream** of ice was seen from the deck, which, as we approached, assumed the appearance of a naval port, extending from south-west to north, as far as the eye could reach. It bore also the semblance of lofty ships, turreted and spired churches, and magnificent buildings. At nine, we ran close to an impenetrable barrier of close-packed ice, composed of massive *hummocks*†, thrown up by some pressure or force, and resembling fragments of rock. Thermometer 14°.

May 6. The wind having changed during the night, I found on coming upon deck, that a gentle breeze from the eastward was taking us to the side of a range of ice, which it was presumed extended to the land, though probably at the distance of one hundred miles. The fineness and beauty of the morning, with still water, yielded a comfort I had scarcely experienced for the last five days; and being relieved from the continuance of that dreadful visitation of sickness, I had leisure to view with delight a bold barrier of ice, grand beyond conception, to one who had never before visited the frozen world. At nine o'clock, a ship under a considerable pressure of sail, crossed our track, as if to be before us in success, and fearlessly went into the ice; four others had been seen to

---

* A number of pieces of ice joined together, forming a continued ridge, and running in any particular direction.

† Pieces of ice thrown up by pressure from large fragments coming in contact.

STREAM OF ICE.

London Pub.d by G.& W.B.Whitaker, Ave Maria Lane.

pass before. It being Sunday, we hauled off to a considerable distance, took in our sails, and lay to, preparatory to the religious observance of the day. It may here be proper to notice that, should a whale be seen close along side the Baffin, on a Sunday, a boat is never lowered down in pursuit.

Scarcely was the morning service ended, when one of the most tremendous gales ever witnessed, began to blow directly towards the ice. The clouds had given no indication of a storm; but, commencing at once with furious blasts, it caused the waves to roll mountains high. We appeared to be the sport of the element: at one instant tossed on its heaving bosom to a frightful height, then descending into a yawning gulf, that threatened to swallow us up; it was nevertheless awfully and sublimely grand. The situation of those ships which we had seen enter the ice in the morning, under what probably was regarded as a propitious gale, was now considered to be so dangerous, that all on board were fearfully apprehensive for their safety. The wind continued raging all the afternoon, with the increased disadvantage of terrific pieces of ice floating about the surface of the ocean: these we had to avoid; and violent snow storms prevented their being seen at any great distance from the ship. About nine o'clock, the gale rather moderated, but as if it had been only to gather strength for an increase of fury; for, during the night, it blew from every point of the compass; which occasioned such a contention of billows, rolling higher and higher, in different directions, as to resemble hillocks coming together with inexpressible rage, and producing overwhelming destruction.

May 7. The gale moderating and settling to the northward, we again sailed towards the ice. It being usual for the officers to dine in the cabin to drink a prosperous voyage, the mate and harpooners were invited this day, and never did I see more justice done to roast beef and plum-pudding! The mirth-inspiring grog made all happy, and the usual fishing toast; "ship strong, crew healthy, ice open, and fish plenty," was drunk by all with great glee. Captain Scoresby, as is usual at this annual meeting, delivered to them his instructions, signals, and particular orders, to be observed when in pursuit of whales; and, as some of them relate to giving assistance to foreign adventurers, and partake so much of the national character, I have procured a copy of them. They will be found, I trust, not unworthy the imitation of other commanders of Greenland ships, and their diffusion may be eminently useful. Latitude this day, 75° 20′; thermometer 27°.

DIRECTIONS TO HARPOONERS WITH REGARD TO ASSISTANCE.

First, "Assist all ships whatever, either British or foreign, when it can be done without disadvantage to your own vessel."

Second, "If you accompany the boat of any ship,

in chase of a fish, and they get fast, if none of their own boats be near, assist them, or bend on, if need be, and remain by them until you be no longer wanted. If you bend on, make no claim for assisting, as no reward will be taken."

Third, "Should you be sent to assist any vessel in killing a fish, do not chase it on any account whatever, if it get loose, but return from the scene of action as soon as possible."

Fourth, "Do not attempt to strike a fish that has just escaped from any ship, provided its boats be in close pursuit; and it is only where a wounded fish is beyond the possible reach of the original striker, that you can be justified in attacking it."

Fifth, "The above conduct, I desire, may be pursued with every ship, whether British or foreign, friendly or unfriendly! if the stranger be a friend, he is entitled to your assistance; if he be one who has withheld his helping hand under like circumstances, your aiding him will shew him his duty in future."

Being aware, from conversation drawn from the harpooners, that a strong jealousy existed respecting the use of the gun-harpoon, and the alterations in the mode of fishing which I had suggested, and intended to make trial of, I considered that, from mismanagement, (without putting any harsher construction upon it,) a useful production is often brought into discredit, by a failure in its first undertaking. I was therefore induced to act with caution, and determined to address them in a tone which might, if possible, remove the hostile impressions, which I both plainly saw, and was confidently assured existed, against my inventions. In addressing them, I stated my object in visiting Greenland, and requested it might be distinctly understood, that it proceeded from no selfish motive, but from a desire to benefit my country, by an endeavour to improve the whale-fishery, and to lessen the dangers that are sometimes fatally attendant on its prosecution; that, for the attainment of these objects, I had devised a hand-harpoon, on a new principle, and felt the greatest confidence, that it would afford better SECURITY in holding the fish, than those now in use; also a gun-harpoon possessing such combined mechanical strength, and singular principles to DEFY RETRACTION; and that I had provided likewise shells and carcasses, to prevent those fatal accidents which often occurred to the crews of boats, in lancing what are termed "*wicked fish.*" The employment of these last missiles, was, I also stated, desirable on the ground of humanity, by their quickly terminating the misery of the fish, and obviating the necessity of the barbarity often unavoidable in the present system, and which had called forth on the whale-fishery, the clamorous indignation of some who possessed the finer feelings of sensibility. I then read the following address to the harpooner appointed to the gun-boat in the presence of the rest.

"Richard Simpkin, you have been selected to the charge and direction of the boat, appointed to try the practical utility of my gun and other apparatus, which are intended to promote and ensure success in the whale-fishery, and to afford assistance, in the time of danger, to those who are prosecuting that service. I only ask for A FAIR and IMPARTIAL TRIAL, to judge whether the adaptation of my inventions to their several intentions, will confirm their utility by practical examples of success, (which I expect that the inveteracy of prejudice cannot withstand,) or whether they will require any alteration or improvement to render them effectual. It is now proper for me to state, that you have been selected, as, this being your first voyage in the rank of harpooner, there is less liability of your being influenced by prejudice, or by an obstinate adherence to old customs.

"I wish you to keep in mind, that my intention is to do an essential public benefit; and in its operation, to obtain advantage to the owners of the ship who give you employment; to your captain who promoted you to the situation of harpooner; to your companions, who are deeply interested in the success of your boat; and lastly, to yourself, not only from the rewards you may acquire from the use of the gun-harpoon, but the credit you will derive in being the first man to establish its utility.

"Let these considerations animate your zeal; let it be ever foremost in your thoughts, that the success of the new system depends upon your own exertions, your collected conduct in the moment of use, and your ability when it is applied; and let these motives induce your particular attention to a branch of service, from which success will never fail to be derived, when the direction of it is skilfully executed."

At eight o'clock, we arrived at the ice, with an intention of entering it, if possible, and I was much struck with the massy pieces that formed the boundary of a deep bight, or bay; one immense hummock was towering above the rest, being in the form of an irregular building, with a considerable hole through it, like a window. On passing the point near this hummock, the appearance of the ice was curious from the irregularity of the pieces which were lying in all directions, in different forms, and of various sizes, like the ruins of some immense city, which had been overthrown by a convulsion of nature. To the westward of the point, another bay presented itself, of about two miles in depth, and four or five to the more distant points; and in the centre was an island with a hummock, at least thirty feet high, resembling a temple. The horizon had a most brilliant appearance from the rays of the sun; and I retired to rest about ten o'clock, leaving it shining about four degrees above the great line of distance.

May 8. I arose about three o'clock, with the expectation that we should enter the ice, but the wind changing again to the south-east, and blowing strong, it was considered not prudent to undertake it: so we sailed off for some hours, and about four o'clock, approached it again, when I was sur-

HUMMOCK RESEMBLING A TEMPLE.

London Pub^d by G. & W.B. Whitaker, Ave Maria Lane.

prised at the great height of many of the pieces, forming extensive pyramids, and a lofty dome, which was observable at some distance. We now entered a bay of ice, about fifteen miles in depth, but the extent of it was beyond the reach of the eye to determine. Its boundary presented an unceasing variety of forms; but those that most arrested my attention, resembled sarcophagi, cromlechs, and that beautiful relic of antiquity on Salisbury plain, Stonehenge. The wind was now blowing a strong breeze; and the working of the ship to clear the large floating incumbrances, with which the bay was studded, was a piece of sailing, that excelled any thing of the kind I had ever before witnessed. At the main topgallant-mast head, the most elevated situation in the ship, a screen of a cylindrical form, termed "*a crow's nest**," was fixed, to afford shelter from the severity of the weather, where, by the command of an extensive view, openings in the ice might be observed, dangers avoided, whales discovered, and movements made in order to enable the ship to attain its destined object. Here our captain took his station in all difficult and arduous situations. At twelve o'clock, having made arrangements for entering the ice, he surveyed the surrounding scene, to discover the most practicable part, which he found to consist of a small neck of ice, about thirty yards in breadth, that separated the ocean from some

---

* The "crow's nest" is often formed and hooped in the manner of a cask.

favourable ice. Having made his decision, he directed the ship to be run within twice or thrice its length of the spot; then promptly ordered the yards a-back, that it might lose all velocity on touching the ice, to break the concussion: again, at the instant of contact, the sails were all filled, and the frozen barrier, no sooner summoned, than its icy gates were forced by the Baffin's prowess. In this manner we entered the ice; and human imagination, to those who had not before witnessed such a scene, cannot conceive any so grand. We now passed into what is professionally called "*open sailing ice**.*" The colour of the water being very favourable for fishing, a good look out was kept, and all were in readiness. We had not proceeded far, before the pieces of ice, which were floating, increased in number and in size; and being of considerable extent and dangerous to pass, every person was at his post, standing by the braces to obey instant command. The wind was blowing strong, the water smooth, and the ship gracefully "danced the hay" in quick time, among numerous dangers, for the distance of thirty or forty miles, when an impenetrable barrier compelled us to put the ship about, and explore other unsearched stations for whales. On passing several large pieces of ice, having apertures, through which light was admitted, a fine effect was produced by the beautiful blue colour, tinted

---

* That is, where the pieces are so separate, as to admit a ship sailing conveniently among them.

SAILING ICE

London Pub'd ... R B Whittaker, Ave Maria Lane.

HUMMOCK OF ICE RESEMBLING A BEAR.

with the richness of ultramarine. This I found to arise from the atmospheric light transmitted through the vacuities of the ice, which possesses the property of decomposing light. Latitude 76° 10′ north.

May 9. The wind having blown extremely hard all night, the ship was brought to, and just at the call of the morning watch, a whale was seen going with great rapidity to windward: four boats were sent in pursuit, but from the great head-sea, the most strenuous exertions proved ineffectual to come up with it. The signal of recall, (a ball at the mizen topmast head,) therefore brought them back again to the ship, without the reward which their efforts merited. We lay to all the day, from a continuance of the south-east gale.

May 10. The wind, which had unceasingly blown, and often with great violence, since the afternoon of the 1st instant, ceased, and, changing to the east, settled to a pleasant breeze. After breakfast, we made sail to windward, through an immense tract, studded with pieces of heavy hummocky ice, bearing a variety of grotesque forms; one, in particular, resembling an immense bear, at least twenty feet high, was uncommonly curious; as we passed, it appeared to be sculptured from the finest statuary marble, and beautifully polished by the action of the waves. The sun was shining with its richest splendour, and so great was its influence in dazzling the eyes, that Captain Scoresby was obliged to leave the crow's nest, to get a pair of green spectacles. The variety of tints displayed on these mountains of ice, from the brightness of the sun on objects so constantly changing their form, would exceed the power of an artist to represent, or of the most fertile imagination to conceive.

To an admirer of the art of sailing, nothing could afford a higher treat than was exhibited this day, in passing through a sea covered with pieces of ice, under a pressure of sail, closely hauled, and going at the rate of eight miles an hour. In one direction, was a stream composed of pieces of ice, closely joined; in another, pieces near each other, through which the ship could only make its way by continual tacking, while immense hummocks threatened our destruction, if we did not respect their consequence by giving way to them. Through these we passed without the slightest accident. It was a most gratifying sight, proving great tractability in the ship, prompt and decisive judgment in the commander, and obedience in the crew; it displayed the perfection of nautical excellence, and convinced me, that the best school to attain practical seamanship, is a Greenland voyage. A considerable swell beginning to be observable, and its consequences being known to produce difficulties and dangers among heavy pieces of ice, this, added to the disappointment of not seeing whales in a place where it was usual to find them, induced us to sail to the westward, to get a new situation. The hemisphere having been cloudless all day, with the sun gloriously illuminating both day and night, I was so struck by the delightful temperature, as to watch, for the purpose of ascertaining the difference of its meridian influence, which was only one degree, the thermometer being 30° at meridian day, and 29° at midnight, if I may so term it.

May 11. The long-wished-for north wind enabled us to make five degrees of east longitude, and to regain the ice in a new situation, where we found the hummocks much larger than I had before seen. The surface of the ocean being only just rippled, I was pleased to observe the effect which a lofty swell had upon those immense bodies of ice: the undulating swell that put them in motion, caused them to rise and fall in the most graceful manner possible. As we proceeded on our eastern course, the pieces of ice increased in size, so as often to shut out the appearance of water at a short distance from the ship. Latitude 76° 11' north.

May 12. Going on deck just as the morning watch was set, I beheld the most magnificent masses of ice, bearing a different character to those I had before seen; they were flat, and of several hundred yards in length and breadth; a vessel, at no great distance from us, was, like ourselves, sailing through them. The weather now began to be much colder, but, although severe, and although the thermometer was much lower than I had at any time seen it in England, the climate was so exhilarating, that its effects were different from those I had ever felt in my native country. The sea was now observed to assume the proper colour of dark water; and more birds being about the ship than had been noticed for many days, and several seals sporting about, I prepared my gun for any subject of natural history that might come near. The ship lying to, I shot a *Columbus Troile*, LINN. The bill was three inches long; the neck, head, back, wings and tail, of a deep mouse-colour; secondaries tipt with white; breast and belly pure white; legs dusky; weight twenty ounces; length seventeen inches; and extent of wing twenty-seven and a half inches. These birds are called the foolish Guillemot, from the stupid indifference they manifest to their own preservation, in exposing themselves to danger. On passing through a continuation of detached pieces of ice, several of them were standing in an erect posture upon them. As we proceeded, the ice became more closely packed, and appeared to set limits to our further progress: the second mate's report from the crow's nest, was to the same effect, and, indeed, the opinion was partly confirmed by three vessels which had been keeping the same course with us, and were now all bearing away. The undismayed commander of the Baffin, whose strong mind acted for itself, and was not influenced by the conduct of others, kept his course, and the ship soon came to some ice of no great resistance, which was separated with ease, causing only a rumbling sound, not unlike distant thunder, or subterraneous matter gathering its materials for a convulsion. Scarcely had the roaring subsided, when the ship struck a large body of ice, which, from the concussion agitated its whole frame with " earthquake shock." It was awful, but inconceivably fine. Having thus forced a passage, we were enabled to keep our course all night.

May 13. The morning was beautifully bright, when we fell in with eight ships, that, like ourselves, had been endeavouring to get to the northward, and spoke one of them, from whom we learned, that neither they nor any other ship they had met with, (though some had been long upon the station,) had seen a whale. Finding the ice to be impenetrable, they all sailed away, with the exception of the Manchester of Hull, whose master came on board to request that Captain Scoresby would allow his surgeon to visit a man under serious indisposition; this was most readily granted, and the surgeon despatched. From the commander of this ship, the following information was obtained: —" that he had been upwards of a month on this station; had spoken many vessels, none of which had seen a whale; and had also found, with them, the ice so close, as to prevent further progress to the north." This, according with the observations which we had made of the extraordinary compactness of the ice, and of the direction in which it was running, confirmed Captain Scoresby in the opinion that it was what is called a close season, with a greater extension of the ice than had occurred for several years. It may here be interesting to point out the distinction between an *open* and a *close* season. The most usual course of the summer ice, which constitutes what is called an open season in the Greenland sea, commences about two degrees south of Cape Farewell, taking thence a north-east direction to Iceland, and then by the side of West Greenland, stretching north-north-east to the north of Jan Mayen, and continuing that course till about the seventy-fourth degree of latitude, which it enters near the sixth degree of east longitude, and from whence it takes a northern direction to the eightieth degree of latitude, leaving an uninterrupted and open passage to the celebrated fishing station, on the western side of Spitzbergen. The character of the present season, is as follows; at the fifteenth degree of west longitude, from Iceland, the ice took a north-east direction, forming a deep bight in the seventy-sixth degree of latitude, in the meridian of Greenwich, and here joining the eastern ice, which probably extended itself to Nova Zembla, if not to Lapland; it consequently shut up the usual passage to the northward, leaving only a space of open sea, on the west side of Spitzbergen, extending round Hakluyt's head-land, terminating round point Look-out, and varying in width a few degrees of longitude. This information was obtained from the masters of some few ships, that were able to penetrate through the ice, by taking a lower degree of latitude than we had attempted.

We kept pursuing our course to the eastward, through very heavy ice, which was singularly attractive, by the extraordinary variety of forms that it exhibited, not unworthy the attention of those fond of architectural studies; having spaces hollowed out, as if formed for the passage of currents, or, as

REMARKABLE PIECE OF ICE RESTING ON COLUMNS.
London. Pub. by G.& W.B.Whittaker, Ave Maria Lane.

if designed as rustic bridges, supported on columns, with regular capitals, most perfectly and beautifully formed. One of these extraordinary forms must have derived the regularity of its parts immediately above the surface, from the vibrating action and friction of the sea lashing those parts within its reach. It was of the following dimensions: pillars above the surface, six feet long; capitals, one foot; the superincumbent mass, from eighteen to twenty feet, and upwards of one hundred feet in width.

The wind ceasing, and a seal being observed on a piece of ice, I requested a boat; but it became alarmed, and I could not get near it; however I shot an *Anas mollissima*, (BUFF.,) or Eiderdrake, of the most beautiful kind. It had a black bill, somewhat elevated; forehead of velvet black: a broad black bar, glossed with purple, extended from thence beyond each eye; middle of the head, whole neck, upper part of the back, scapulas, and coverts of the wings, white; below the hind part of the head, a stain of pea-green; lower part of the back, tail, breast, and whole under side of the body, black; legs, greenish; weight, seven pounds; length, two feet two inches; and extent of wing, three feet. Nature having clothed this species of birds with the warmest covering of down, their skin is rendered so exceedingly valuable that it forms a considerable article of commerce from Iceland. They dive to a great depth, and keep under water an astonishing time. They are supposed not to arrive at their full plumage until five years of age, and live very long.

May 15. The difficulties, which we expected to meet with in keeping our course, accumulated as the ice became more compact and the pieces much larger; the face of the ocean being often totally excluded from our sight by the immense bodies floating on its surface. I could not help beholding with wonder and delight, the movements of the ship through them; it now being deemed necessary to have recourse to *boring* the ice, that is, forcing a passage through large bodies of it. The address requisite was very interesting; and nothing but the most skilful seamanship, and prompt obedience of the ship to the movements of the helm, could effect what came under my observation. I went to the bows to observe the tactics employed in facing the enemy, and was much gratified by the judicious mode of attack. To meet an immense surface of ice, perhaps fifty times the ship's superior in weight, in hasty advance or in front, would be ineffectual; therefore, on approaching it, the rapid movement of the ship was progressively checked, until the bow was introduced between two of the pieces, and at the instant of contact, the whole power of the sails was applied to force aside the obstruction. During the day we passed several fragments of *ice-bergs**, that probably had been the growth of ages, and were of the richest

---

* Insulated mountains of ice.

hue of dense blue ice. In cases where the pieces that opposed our progress were not very ponderous, a contention for strength was often to determine the issue; and the struggle, in some instances, was considerable, but the power of the ship being so judiciously and mechanically applied, made the ice yield in the contest, so that we invariably forced a passage. Boats were now got out a-head, to assist the ship to keep her course. The ice gathering very fast, ice poles were used for forcing openings, while the boats went a-head, to try which pieces might be the most easily removed. In this manner we went two or three miles, until a barrier of solid ice, many leagues in breadth, rendered it impossible to proceed any further. The ice through which we had passed, being observed to be rapidly closing, the promptest decision was necessary; and immediate exertion, it was evident, could alone save us from being locked in by the ice, probably for several weeks, and thereby losing the season for fishing. A moment was not to be lost; the ship's head was got round, to retrace her former course; and it was most fortunate that the quick determination to retire was carried into effect; as a stiff breeze springing up, caused the ice to close so very fast, that half an hour later would have prevented our escape. On clearing our difficulties, we sailed to the north-west.

At one period of the day, when the ship could make its passage without the assistance of the boat, I had some excellent shooting; killing upwards of twenty specimens of the *little Auk*. These birds fly with great swiftness against the wind, and waver from side to side in their flight, like snipes. I was much amused at the pleasure expressed by the boat's crew, on seeing me kill twelve of these swift-winged birds, without missing. They have a short, black, convex and thick bill, its upper part black; cheeks, and lower part, white; legs, dirty greenish white; webs, black; head and neck, black; weight, five ounces; length, nine inches; extent of wing, fifteen inches. They dive wonderfully quick, frequently putting their beak to the water, as if to drink. They live on shrimps, many of which I took from the stomach: their voice is singular, resembling the forced laugh of punch in a puppet-show.

May 16. This morning I came on deck at four o'clock, and was much gratified by a remarkable bright land blink, and by the sight of our destined northern object, Spitsbergen, which was

to the eastward of us, about thirty or forty miles. We were not near enough distinctly to discover the nature of the coast, more than its lofty mountains in the vicinity of Horn Sound, whose summits, crowned with eternal snow, towered some into the clouds, and others above them. It was however sufficiently near to present a picture of extreme dreariness and desolation, full of craggy mountains and deep glens. The first discovery of these islands extending from the seventy-sixth to the eighty-first parallel of north latitude, was made by Barentz in 1594.

From the gale in the night, the ice had collected around us, so that we were in a basin; to get out of which, much display of seamanship was exhibited. The difficulties of yesterday were nothing in comparison to those with which we had now to contend; the pieces of ice were, if possible, more numerous, more closely packed, and of the rockiest hardness. To discover a passage from the entanglement was attempted at every point of the compass; but finding twenty-eight of the thirty-two points to be impenetrable, every address which the ablest judgment could suggest, was not only necessary but employed for the purpose, our situation being so very critical. I spent much time at the head of the ship, to observe the operations, and beheld with admiration the caution and resolution displayed. The ice being of a nature requiring the most prudential choice of attack, it not only appeared conscious of its own power, but, as though determined to succeed, had collected a host of auxiliaries to impede our progress. The ship was equally prepared for the combat, and its skilful commander placed himself at the mast head, to observe the movements of the enemy, and to take the best position: pieces of ice of such immense magnitude and weight, as, it might be imagined, must overwhelm us, often opposed our progress: to meet these, was displayed nautical skill, interesting beyond description; such as when advancing, under a pressure of sail, promptly bracing back the yards in an instant to impede the ship's way; then, at the moment of meeting, filling the sails, and driving the obstinate foe aside. Numbers of the finest evolutions were made during the day; we turned with celerity upon the flanks of some, upon the rear of others, and on many occasions manœuvered in the perfect figure of 8, to defeat not only the columns, but the reserves that threatened to cut off our retreat, and keep us captive in a prison of ice, if not to effect our destruction. By the uncommon perseverance of Captain Scoresby, who remained thirteen hours in the crow's nest, the thermometer being twelve degrees below the freezing point, we were at eleven e'clock at night, once again in the open sea, to explore and pursue some more favourable situation for fishing; for which purpose we sailed to the north-west. At one period of the day, when the wind had ceased, and the difficulties were less formidable, I requested a boat to examine some bodies of ice at no great distance from us. On approaching them, nothing could exceed their endless variety, elegance of shape, and apparent execution, as if just from the hands of the sculptor. They were of the densest ice, of transparent blue, and as hard as marble. Some represented vases, which for classical structure, might have done credit to the taste of the artist; indeed, I am persuaded of the advantage that would arise to the fine arts among us, if an artist of taste were to take accurate sketches of the endless variety exhibited in the arctic seas. On my return to the ship, I killed several birds, already described; and two of the *Lari eburnei*, Ivory-gulls or snow-birds. The bill and lip of this gull, is of lead colour; length, from the tip of the beak to the end of the tail, sixteen inches; extent of wings, thirty-seven inches. This beautiful bird is seldom seen far from the ice, and is of the purest white, the primaries being slightly tinged with pink; the eye large, jet-black and sparkling, fringed, with a crimson lid. Lat. 77° North. Saw several Greenland doves, *Columbus Grylle*, LINN., and one, strange to say, settled on the fore-top-gallant-yard, and was caught by a seaman. Its length, fourteen inches; extent of wing, twenty-two inches; weight, fifteen ounces; the bill black, slender, and pointed; the whole plumage, glossy black, except a large patch of white on the coverts of the wings.

May 17. In consequence of some fresh difficulties occurring during the night, and the season being late for getting to the north, it was now considered prudent to abandon our intention of going to Spitzbergen; a resolve which I really regretted, as I anticipated much satisfaction in collecting, for the advancement of natural history, various specimens of animal, vegetable, and mineral productions, from a part of the arctic regions, which has of late so much engaged public attention. My regret was also excited in being deprived of the opportunity of visiting its celebrated ice-bergs, renowned among the principal wonders of the polar world. I felt likewise the greatest disappointment as a sportsman, in not taking with my own hands, some of those ferocious quadrupeds which abound there, and the different species of birds, which assemble in such great numbers, particularly ducks and snipes. By Captain Scoresby's kind consent, I here extract from his journal, his reasons for not proceeding further northward.

"Having failed in discovering either fish or a passage to the northward, in any meridian in east longitude, though we tried to the utmost in several places, we proceeded on the seventeenth of May to the north-west, until we fell in with the western ice. The wind then blowing strong from the north, we plied all night, among streams and patches of ice, to windward; the officer of the watch having orders to work to the north-east, that we might, on a new meridian, about that of London, examine whether there was not an opening leading to the usual fishing-stations, lying further north. By some blunder, however, instead of plying to the north-east, the ship's course was directed to the north-west, so that, on my visiting the deck, I found the

FRAGMENT OF AN ICE BERG.

London. Pub. by G. & W.B.Whittaker, Ave Maria Lane.

ship almost surrounded with compact ice, and no great prospect of advancing much further to the northward. As such, the usual time for the commencement of the southern fishing being near, we tacked, and stood to the south-west, expecting in that direction to gain the open sea, near the place where we entered; but instead of this, we got more and more involved, and found the ice quite impervious in the N. NE. E. SE. S. SW. W. and all round as far as the NW. the points intermediate between NW. and N. being the only practicable tract. We were therefore obliged to stand back to the N., until we rounded a point of ice; then, after steering E. SE. and S. a distance of twenty or twenty-five miles, we were enabled to haul out to the SW., a course which, if my orders had been obeyed, should have led us out from our position in the morning."

Proceeding on our south-west course, we passed through occasional streams of ice, of considerable extent, and a few fragments of ice-bergs, one of which was particularly remarkable, being upwards of one hundred and fifty feet in length, and fifty feet from the surface of the water, having apertures like windows. Another at a distance resembled a tower, seated upon an immense base, of very considerable height, at least seventy feet, of a most beautiful berylline blue, and nearly perpendicular.

May 18. We sailed into a bight of about ten miles across, surrounded on twenty-four points of the compass, from south-west by north to south-east, with ice. Here we lay to, as a strong gale from the north-east enabled the ship to keep in a quiet situation; and, as it was a wind best suited to open the ice to the northward, we might proceed, should circumstances yet occur, to a greater latitude without much loss of time. The gale continuing, we kept our situation during the nineteenth, twentieth, and twenty-first: the latter day being Sunday, the crew attended the usual divine service, consisting of prayers and an excellent sermon.

The gale having abated, under the presumption that it might have opened a passage we sailed to the north-west, for about five hours, when, not being able to proceed any longer in that direction, and the blue colour of the water being still discouraging, we sailed to the south-west, into a bight, in which were streams of ice with very heavy hummocks upon them. Feelings of disappointment, at not having seen any whales, were now apparent in every countenance: I shared in them most sensibly, and retired to my cabin, to bury my annoyance in sleep, in which I had not indulged more than an hour or two, when I was aroused by the joyful sound of "A fish!! Lower away the boats!"; and the greatest imaginable bustle prevailed upon the deck. No mind can possibly conceive the momentary transition effected on my spirits, at the idea that the time was at length arrived, when, from practical observation, I should be able to form a decided opinion, whether my inventions for an improved method of taking whales were adapted to their design, or, if not, what was required to render them effective. When I arrived on the deck, the whale had gone down; and the ship was going in the direction of its last appearance, but in a few minutes, this monster of the deep, rose again, not three hundred yards from us. From the pointed part of the head, termed the crown, where the spiracles or blow-holes are situated, a moist vapour was emitted to the height of several yards, and was accompanied by a noise, not unlike that of a powerful furnace blast.

A long extent of the back was also exhibited, just above the surface of the water. After having rested in this state about three minutes, during which time it took several respirations, it reared its ponderous head, then sinking it under the water, raised its back, at least six feet, in the form of an arch, rounding it towards the extremity,

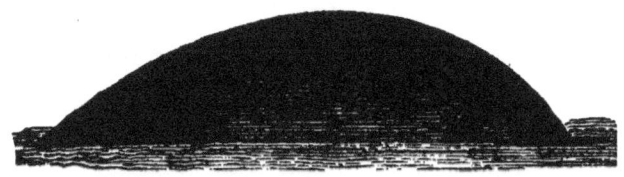

and elevating its extensive tail, with a graceful curvature of movement, sunk into the deep.

It may here be proper to observe, that, from the improbability of seeing a whale, in a situation without either favourable water or ice, and from the sportive manner of its retiring, the experienced on board inferred that it had a young one with it; for whales often retire to some situation, unfrequented by other whales, for the purpose of giving early exercise to their young. In a short time the whale rose again, when a hand-harpoon was thrown at it as it was descending, but without effect; and here the advantage of a gun-harpoon was self-evident, as the distance was certainly not a boat's length. Boats now were disposed in various stations, ready again to assail it on its re-ascent to breathe, but probably the harpoon having touched it, it became alarmed, as it was seen no more. The boat appropriated to carry my gun did not go; the harpooner appointed to it being by illness confined to his birth.

It was now discovered, that the opinion of the experienced was correct, and that the whale we had seen was attending on its offspring, or instructing it to provide for itself, by collecting sustenance, and by swimming for protection to situations among ice, where man could least annoy it. But probably, having lost its affectionate tutor, in consequence of the alarm given to it by the harpooner, or not being sufficiently instructed in the laws of self-preservation, the young fish, as with no consciousness of danger in its unoffending nature, rose near a boat, the harpooner of which knew no distinction or merit in a whale beyond the quantity of oil it would yield; he immediately plunged his weapon into the back, and with the assistance of others, soon killed it, and brought it to the ship. Captain Scoresby taking an earnest interest in subjects relating to natural history, ordered it to be hoisted up, and laid upon the deck, that its structure might be the more minutely examined. It measured nineteen feet in length, and fourteen feet five inches in circumference; the longest laminæ of whalebone were twelve inches. The general appearance of the animal was particularly uncouth, and I was much amazed at the extreme disproportion of those different organs, the head, the eye, and the ear.

Being the common Greenland whale, a description of its peculiarities, as well as some account of the early state of the fishing, may not be unacceptable.

By Linnæus, the whale is called *Balæna*, a name derived from a Greek word expressive of the great power it possesses to cast up water. It forms a genus of the class *Mammalia*, and order *Cete;* and, although it is an inhabitant of the water, it is classed with the quadrupeds, which it resembles in suckling its young, in breathing air, and in having warm blood and flesh composed of animal substance, as well as in being also furnished with lungs, and with other parts of a similar structure to those of land animals.

The *Balæna Mysticetus*, the Greenland whale, has no fin upon its back; the head is one third the size of the fish; the lips are quite smooth, and very elastic, and the under one much broader than the upper, turning in this form ⌒ and ending before the fins; the under side of the lower lip is beautifully white, and has small black spots, from each of which grows a single hair; the eyes are placed just above the end of the upper lip, and in size do not exceed those of an ox; they are very bright, and well calculated to see in the medium, through which the light has to pass: they consist of a crystalline lens, not larger than a pea, and are guarded by lids and brows, like human eyes: the organs of hearing are placed behind the eyes: they are most minute circular orifices, without any projecting external appendages, which might embarrass the animal in its natural element, each having an auditory canal about the size of a quill, leading to the seat of hearing; but it does not possess that sense in an ex-

traordinary degree, as it is not at any great distance
alarmed at the noise of danger preparing for it: on
the top of the head is the protuberance, termed the
crown, in the front of which are two orifices for the
convenience of respiration. Through these it ejects
its breath with a degree of force, that often makes
it appear like water: they are placed in the part
that, in the natural progress of motion, comes first
to the surface of the water; the fins are articulated,
and placed a little behind that part of the mouth,
where the jaw-bones terminate; their use seems to
be to give steadiness in the water by balancing the
animal, for, as soon as life is extinct, it falls on its
side or turns on its back; with the fins it also affords
protection to its young; behind these is the thickest
part, which is cylindrical; and this form continues
to some distance, and decreases like a cone towards
the tail. The tail is the formidable weapon, from
which the whale derives its astonishing strength
for motion and defence: by means of this, it advances through the ocean, and the greatest velocity
is produced by powerful strokes against the water,
impelled alternately upward or downward. To give
a slow motion, the tail cuts the water laterally and
obliquely downward, in the manner of an oar when
used at the stern of a boat, in what is called "skul-
ling." The position of the tail is horizontal, in-
dented in the middle; it has two lobes, pointed, and
turned rather backward, and is composed of sinewy
fibres, with two large layers of tendons, leading both
above and below, from the back and belly of the

fish, to the upper and lower indentations. The tail and fins are covered with skin like that on the other parts of the body; but internally they widely differ from it, the body having blubber under the skin, but the tail and fins being a combination of strong cartilages. The skin of the Mysticetus is very smooth, and slightly furrowed, like the water-marks in paper: it varies in colour; being, when young, of a bluish black, but, when the fish is full grown, black. On some, towards the tail, are brown spots on a light ground; some have white round the eyes, and streaks of white on the fins and different parts of the body, whilst others are much and irregularly spotted. The organs of generation are placed near that part of the abdomen, where the body begins to taper suddenly towards the tail; that of the male, is concealed in a longitudinal groove. The teats or nipples are placed on each side of the female organ, and are not capable of protrusion, beyond an inch or two; in a dead fish they are always retracted. The sexual intercourse takes place about the end of summer, and once in two years the fish feels the access of desire. Their fidelity to each other, exceeds even the constancy of birds. Anderson, a celebrated whale-fisher, informs us, that "having struck one of two whales, a male and a female, that were in company together, the wounded fish made a long and terrible resistance: it struck down a boat with three men in it, by a single blow of its tail, and they all went to the bottom. The other remained with its companion, and rendered it every assistance, till, at length, the fish that was struck, sunk under the number of its wounds; while its faithful associate, disdaining to survive the loss, stretched itself with great bellowing, upon the dead fish, and shared its fate."

The whale goes with young nine or ten months, and is then fatter than usual, particularly when near the time of bringing forth. It is said, that the embryo, when first perceptible, is about seventeen inches long, and white; but the young fish at its birth is black, and about ten feet long. The mother generally produces one at a time, but never exceeds two; and in suckling, she throws herself on one side, on the surface of the water. Nothing can surpass the tender attachment and maternal attention which a female whale will sometimes manifest, if her young one be harpooned: she joins it at the surface, whenever it has occasion to rise for respiration, encourages it to swim off, assists its flight by taking it under her fin, and seldom deserts it while life remains. She is then dangerous to approach: but affords frequent opportunities for attack. She loses all regard for her own safety, in anxiety for the preservation of her young; dashes through the midst of her enemies; despises the dangers that threaten her; and even voluntarily remains with her offspring, after various attacks on herself from the harpoons of the fishers. An extraordinary instance of this is related by Captain Scoresby:—" In June, 1811, one of my harpooners struck a sucker, with the hope of its leading to the capture of the mother. Presently she arose close to the fast boat, and, seizing, the young one, dragged out of the boat about one hundred fathoms of line, with remarkable force and velocity; again she arose to the surface, darted furiously to and fro, frequently stopped short and suddenly changed her direction, and gave every possible indication of extreme agony. For a length of time she continued to act thus, although closely pursued by the boats; and, inspired with courage and resolution for the welfare of her offspring, seemed regardless of the dangers which surrounded herself. At length, one of the boats approached so near, that a harpoon was thrown at her: it struck, but did not attach itself; a second was thrown; this also failed; but a third was more effectual, and yet she did not attempt to escape, but allowed three other boats to approach, so that, in a few minutes, three more harpoons were fastened, and in the space of an hour afterwards she was killed."

The young ones continue to suck for a year, during which period they are called by the sailors, *short-heads*. They are then extremely fat, and yield above thirty barrels of blubber. The mother, on the other hand, becomes at that time proportionately lean and emaciated. At the age of two years, the young are called *stunts*, as they do not thrive much immediately after quitting their parent; they then yield scarcely above twenty or twenty-four barrels of blubber: after this they are called *skull-fish*, and their age is wholly unknown. Every species of whale propagates only with those of its own kind, and does not mingle at all with the rest; though they are generally seen in shoals of different kinds together, and migrate in large companies from one ocean to another. The Mysticetus has no teeth, but merely laminæ, or, what is known by the name of *whale-bone*, ranged in the upper jaw, in two rows, similar to those found in the bill of the duck: they occupy precisely the place of the teeth in other animals, are set with the greatest regularity, and vary in length and breadth, according to the size of the fish, being in a large fish, upwards of thirteen feet in length; they are attached to the crown bone, and are placed in a longitudinal direction along the middle of the upper jaw: in number, they are upwards of two hundred on each side, and are fastened in a soft elastic white substance, called the gum. The upper part of the jaw also resembles the upper mandible of a duck: it is smooth, and of a glossy black. The interior edge of the laminæ is covered with hair, not unlike that of a horse: this, nature has provided for the purpose of preserving the tongue of the animal from injury, as well as to enable it the better to secure its prey, by preventing its return with the water ejected from its nostrils. When seeking food, the whale swims with considerable velocity beneath the surface of the water, with its capacious mouth extended; in the closed mouth the fringed parts of the laminæ form a net, that will not allow the animalculæ on which it feeds to escape. The tongue is an immense mass, covering the whole lower surface of the mouth, and is partly blubber and partly krang*, intermixed: near the tip it chiefly consists of the former; much blubber is also procured from the other extremity.

In inquiring into the origin of the British whale trade, it is observable that it was late before our nation engaged in the fishery; for it appears that, in the year 1575, we were totally ignorant of the trade, being obliged to send to " Biskaie for men skilful in the catching of the whale, and ordering of the oil, and one cooper skilful to set up the staved cask." This seems very strange; as in the account given by Octher to King Alfred of his travels, near seven hundred years before that period, he made that monarch acquainted with the Norwegian practice of the whale-fishery; but it seems, that all memory of that advantageous branch of commerce, as well as of Octher and of all his important discoveries in the north, was lost for nearly seven centuries. The trade was carried on by the Biscayans, long before it was attempted by the English; and that, for the sake not only of the oil, but also of the whale-bone, in which they seem long to have dealt. The earliest notice we find of that article in our own trade, is by Hackluyt, who says, " it was brought from the Bay of St. Lawrence by an English ship that went there for barbes and fynnes of whales and train oil, A. D. 1594, and who

---

* Krang is a name given by fishermen to the fleshy part, after the blubber is taken off.

found there seven hundred or eight hundred whalefynnes, part of the cargo of two great Biskaine ships, that had been wrecked there three years before."
Previously to that time, ladies' stays must have been made of split cane, or some tough wood, as Mr. Anderson observes in his *Dictionary of Commerce;* it being certain that the whale-fishery was pursued for the sake of the oil, long before the use of whalebone was ascertained. The great resort of these animals was found to be on the inhospitable shores of Spitzbergen; the European ships therefore made that their principal place of fishery, and for a number of years were very successful: the English commenced the business in 1598, and the town of Hull had the honour of first attempting so profitable a branch of trade. At present, it seems to be on the decline, the quantity of fish being greatly reduced by the constant capture during such a vast length of time: some recent accounts inform us, that the fishers, from a defect of whales, apply themselves to the seal-fishery, from which animals they extract an oil. This it is to be feared will not be of very long continuance; for these shy and timid creatures will soon be induced to quit those shores, by being perpetually harassed; as, indeed, the walrus has in a great measure already done. We are also told, that the poor natives of Greenland begin even now to suffer from the diminished number of seals in their seas, these fish being their principal subsistence; so that, should they totally desert the coast, the whole nation would be in danger of perishing through

want. In ancient times, the whale seems never to have been taken on our coasts, but when it was accidentally thrown ashore by some violent storm or tempest: it was then deemed a royal fish, and, according to legendary history, the king and queen divided the spoil; the king asserting his right to the head, and her majesty to the tail.

On opening the whale we had killed, an extremely thin epidermis or scarf skin covered the main skin, which resembles solid Indian rubber, of a pale blue colour, soft and easily cut, and of an inch in thickness: beneath it, the blubber, which subjects this inoffensive creature to such persecution, was five inches and a half deep; in this substance, the oil is retained, in the same manner as a sponge retains water, and it yields to compression: in a large fish, it is eighteen or twenty inches thick. Next to the blubber lay a thin stratum of extremely tough and stringy white fibres; under this, the muscular membrane and krang surround the cavity of the abdomen containing the intestines. The quantity of blood that flowed from the animal was very great, and prevented a close investigation of the intestines. The temperature of the blood was 100°: the flesh resembled beef, and was far from uninviting to the taste; but in an old fish it is black, and very coarse: the liver was like that of other animals, but not so firm in texture: the heart was a firm fleshy substance, having two ventricles and two auricles, with immense cavities for the different blood-vessels; it was flat and broad, and weighed sixty-four pounds:

the quantity of the intestines was extremely great, and their convolutions arranged in a manner similar to those of other animals, and filled with a milky substance drawn from its mother: the kidneys were flat and conglomerated, and composed of small parts, which, from their evenness, being under a filament, had the appearance of pavements placed close together. The principal interior organs of hearing were curious in the extreme; the bones resembled shells.

Near the throat a valve of extraordinary structure was discovered, which, I regret, was much injured by the unskilful hands of a harpooner: it is not improbable that this beautiful valve was a connecting part of that noble economy of nature for forcing the air through the blow-holes, in the upper surface of the head. The fins were exquisitely adapted to their purpose; underneath the skin, the bones were formed and placed like those of a man's hand, with the fingers expanded: these bones had joints connected by strong sinews, which rendered them so strong, that, if bent, they would fly back with great force to their original extension.

The cavity containing the brains was placed behind the crown in the head, and very small in proportion to the size of the fish; the crown-bone, and the bones of the upper jaw, like most of the other bones of the whale, were very porous, and contained a considerable quantity of oil.—Having finished the dissection, and taken drawings of the various parts of the animal, I retired to my cabin at twelve o'clock at night, with the sun shining in all the splendour of meridian day.

May 24. The wind blowing very strong, we sailed to the north-west, in readiness to enter the western ice as soon as the gale should abate, and an opening be discovered; about noon, the wind became moderate and we sailed to the west, and at three o'clock, came to the great range of ice: on approaching it, the man at the mast-head intimated that a herd of seals were upon the ice. Two boats were lowered, and we went in pursuit of them, when I shall never forget the extraordinary sight which was presented on our approaching the spot. There were many hundred seals upon one piece of ice, and they literally covered its surface; some lying asleep at their full length, others playfully stretched in an infinite variety of postures: when the boats arrived within one hundred yards of them, the alarm was given, for some of a herd are always on the watch: they instantly reared themselves to give us a look, then hurried to the edge of the ice as fast as their inaptness for travelling would permit, and plunged into the water. The animals presented a whimsical scene of confusion as they tumbled about and overturned each other in the attempt to escape. The men in the boat wished me not to use my gun, stating that they had furnished themselves with clubs, with which they could kill plenty: but the agility of these amphibious animals eluded the activity of their pursuers, and was astonishing, considering the shortness of their legs, and the great exertion by which their movements were effected: only one was procured. On a piece of ice yet further, about twenty more were seen reposing; and, having now full as much faith in my gun as in the activity of the boat's crew, I singled out one of the handsomest, (marked by a bright arrangement of various colours,) that was marching away in double quick time, and lodged a charge of small shots in his black pug nose: thus he was easily secured; the boat's crew also caught one, after it had made great efforts to save its life, by endeavouring to bite every one that approached it.

These animals are the *Phoca vitulina* of Linnæus: in the scale of nature they are intermediate between amphibious animals and perfect fish, but partake more of the latter than of the former; as Buffon remarks, " they are the only animals that have the *foramen ovale* open, and that can therefore live without respiring: and to whom water is as proper and suitable an element as air." The *Phoca vitulina* has a large flat head; a short nose, like a pug dog; strong and sharp teeth; no external appearance of ears, but merely an aperture to convey the sound; eyes small, and of a haggard appearance: neck short, and thickening as it approaches the shoulders, which are the largest part of the animal. Hence the body regularly tapers in a cylindrical form to the extremity, where are placed the hind legs, between which is a very short tail: the fore paws or flippers consist of five fingers, joined together by a membrane, and ending in sharp and strong claws: the hind paws are like them, except the fingers, which are somewhat longer. Seals are covered with coarse short hair, varying much in different individuals of the species; among those I first saw, was one perfectly white, whilst others were beautifully marked with spots of black, red, and liver colour, of greater or less magnitude. This animal is gregarious, and feeds on fish: its length is about five feet. Seals are found in the greatest abundance on the ice, in the vicinity of the island of Jan Mayne, early in the spring; when, in fine weather, they prefer lying on the ice to being in the water. They are extremely watchful; for, as already observed when a number are collected together, some are always on the alert, to give the alarm in case of danger. It is presumed that they adopt this precaution, to guard them against their grand enemy, the polar bear, on whose approach, the greatest dread is apparent, by the confusion in which they hurry to escape into the water. The seal-fishing in Greenland was formerly a considerable branch of commerce to foreign nations; but the British regard it as of little importance, because, at the season of the year when these animals congregate, the exposed situations where they abound, are liable to sudden and violent storms: the following melancholy narrative of an event, that occurred in the year 1774, is recorded by a pilot, who was an eye-witness of the fact.

" Fifty-four ships, chiefly Hamburghers, were that year fitted out from foreign ports, for the seal-fishing alone: most of these, with several English ships, had, in the spring of the year, met together on the borders of the ice, about sixty miles to the eastward of the island, Jan Mayne. On the twenty-ninth of March, the weather being moderate, the whole fleet penetrated within some streams of ice, and sent out their boats in search of seals. While they were thus engaged, a dreadful storm suddenly arose; so sudden and furious indeed was its commencement, and so tremendous and lasting its continuance, that almost all the people that were at a distance from their ships perished. A ship, named the Duke of York, had two boats out at this time; the crews of these having, by the utmost exertion, rowed up to the ship, held fast by the rudder-rings, being unable to make their way along side; here they remained for some time, but, at length, the force of the waves becoming too great for their benumbed grasp, they lost their hold, and drove astern. The chief mate of the ship, a resolute and noble tar, seeing that his shipmates, if not immediately succoured, would perish, determined to rescue them at the hazard of his own life. Having manned a boat with six stout seamen, besides himself, he proceeded to their assistance. On reaching them, he exchanged four of his vigorous crew for two of his fainting ship-mates in each boat; thus reinforced, the three boats by the powerful exertions of their crews, were brought to the stern of the ship. Beyond this point the increase of the waves, and the rapid drift of the ship, prevented their advancing, while their companions on board were unable to assist them, all their attention being requisite for their own preservation; as the ship lay almost on her beam ends. In this critical situation they had not remained many minutes, when a wave struck the boats, filled and overwhelmed them, and the whole of the crews, nineteen in number, perished. But this catastrophe, melancholy as it was, formed only a small proportion of the disasters of the storm.

"While the different ships were endeavouring to make their way clear of the ice, the ship, Pennant, was struck by so dreadful a surge, that it foundered, and all the crew perished; the same wave struck the ships, Perseverance and Rockingham, by which one of the quarter-boats of the latter was thrown upon the deck, and the bulwark, fore and aft, was washed away; five boats and five men were washed from the sides and deck of the former, while at the same time, such damage was occasioned to the hull of the ship, that it was under the necessity of returning home to refit. A Dutch snow, on board of which the crews of six English boats had taken refuge, falling to leeward against a point of ice, was wrecked, and all on board perished. It was estimated that, during this dreadful gale, about four hundred foreign seamen, and nearly two hundred British, were drowned, and four or five ships totally lost; scarcely any escaped without damage."

To return from this digression to the more immediate account of our proceedings, we had not sailed more than an hour or two into the ice after the capture of the young whale, before the water assumed the colour known to be the favourite resort of whales, and soon after, a fish being seen, boats were sent in pursuit; the mate threw a harpoon at it, but without effect, it being eight or nine yards from him. All were now looking out, and I retired to my cabin at twelve o'clock, and, as usual, slept in my clothes, in anxious expectation of soon being roused by the noise of war with the mighty animal of whom we were in quest.

May 25. At three o'clock my expectation was realized, for I was disturbed by such a noise, bustle, and confusion, that, had I not been acquainted with the cause, I should naturally have imagined, either that the crew had mutinied, the ship was on fire, or some inevitable destruction fast approaching. I arose and went on deck, and saw near us a boat with its jack flying, as a signal that a whale had been stricken; the watch were stamping on the deck like madmen, while others, running to their separate boats, were exclaiming "a fall! a fall!" that is, a fish is fast, and all must turn out in pursuit. This welcome summons brought the remainder of the crew instantly upon the deck, when it was truly ludicrous to see them come from below, in their shirts, just as they had left their births, with their clothes under their arms, hurrying to their boats to dress themselves in them, whilst they were lowered from the cranes that suspended them over the sides of the ship. The boats soon repaired towards the scene of action, and were arranged in different places ready for the attack ; on the re-appearing of the fish several harpoons were plunged into it, and it was quickly despatched by the lances. From the feeble resistance it made, it was evidently not of magnitude, or possessing much strength. It proved to be a female whale, twenty-seven feet in length, and eighteen feet six inches in circumference.

After the necessary arrangements of securing the fins, the fish was fastened by the tail to a boat, and towed to the ship, for the purpose of " flincing," or stripping it of its blubber, which is performed in the following manner: tackles being fixed to the nose and tail, the fish, with the belly upper most (as here represented), is secured along-side of the ship ; the harpooners, with their spurs*, getting on the fish, make parallel incisions through the substance of the blubber, about three feet asunder, and in a transverse direction ; they next raise a large flap, in the centre of which they cut a hole large enough to admit the

* Spiked irons, secured to the bottom of their boots to prevent their slipping.

strap of the main tackle, called a kant; the use of which is to turn the body of the fish, as the flincing advances; large masses are then cut off until the whole operation is finished, and each piece hoisted in by persons at the capstan, who, in the present instance, cheered every heaving with a merry extempore song, which excited much mirth, and kept all the men in good humour, while they united their strength by stepping to the tune. The belly part being finished, the whole was turned round by the kant, and the tackles fastened to the fins for flincing that part, which could not be done as it was first placed. Each mass, on being lowered on the deck, was cut into square pieces by the boat-steerers, and thrown into the hold, where others were employed in stripping off the unproductive part from the blubber. The whale-bone, jaw-bones, and whatever was valuable in the head, having been hoisted on board, the body, with all its appurtenances, was cut away from the tackles, and descended to the bottom of the deep.

A whale is estimated by the extent of its laminæ or whale-bone, and, consequently this capture promised but little advantage to the owners, the bone measuring only four feet. It was presumed to be about four years old. The process of flincing being finished, the decks were cleared and cleaned. Captain Scoresby, whose indefatigable zeal ever kept him on the look out, saw from the mast-head, three whales lying together to windward, and one at the same time was seen to leeward of us; the usual bustle took place, and boats were sent in pursuit, from one of which, by some mismanagement, the harpooner made an ineffectual throw, which frightened away the whales, and they were seen no more. In the return of one of the boats, a unicorn, or narwal was killed, and brought to the ship: it measured fourteen feet in length, and the horn four feet two inches.

The head of the narwal is about one-fourth the length of the body, round, small, and terminating in an obtuse nose; mouth small; no teeth; eyes small and nearly oval; external opening of the ear a minute orifice. The orifices for respiration in the back part of the head duplicated within, and with a structure exquisitely formed, have the appearance of human lips; back broad, convex, and tapering towards the tail, which is horizontal; the pectoral fins small, and bending inwards; colour generally cinereous, dappled with numerous black spots; belly shining white, and soft as velvet. It does not yield much blubber, which is only three inches and a half in thickness; between the blubber and the muscles, is a range of tendons along the back, some of them as small as the finest thread. The narwal is a native of the northern seas, where it is sometimes seen of the length of more than twenty feet, from its mouth to the tail, and is distinguishable from every other kind of whale, by its very long horn-like tooth, which is perfectly straight, smooth, and of a yellowish white colour, spirally wreathed throughout its whole length, invariably twisting from left to right, and gradually tapering to a sharp point. This tusk, which is from one to nine or ten feet long, proceeds from a socket on the left side of the upper jaw, and is usually hollow from the base to a considerable extent. It is regarded as the finest ivory, and was formerly numbered among the articles of regal magnificence. A throne, made of such for the Danish monarch, is still preserved in the castle of Rosenburg, and is considered by the possessors to be of more value than gold. Besides this tusk or horn, which is peculiar to the male, there is another on the right side of the head, imbedded in the skull; this latter is solid throughout, and placed back in the substance of the skull, about six inches from the most prominent part. The skull of the narwal is concave above, having a flat, wedge-shaped, large projection in front, which affords sockets for the tusks; the cavity in the head, that communicates with the blowholes, is divided by a bony substance. In the hollow of the ear are occasionally found large bunches of worms, about an inch and a half long, constantly in motion, and as fine as very small sewing thread. The narwal is very active, and swims with great swiftness, but cannot keep under the water long. Before the fish comes to the surface to respire, a strange tremulous hurried noise is heard: they generally rise in little herds, and make a feeble blast in the direction over their nose. The food of the narwal consists of the sepia or cuttle-fish, many of which I took from the stomach of this specimen. Just as we were finishing the examination of the narwal, a whale was seen to blow at a great distance: six boats were immediately sent off, but as they were not able to overtake it, the signal of recall was made, and five of them returned. On the arrival of the first, I went into it with my gun, for the purpose of shooting a remarkable snow-bird with a black head, which came near the ship: this with two others I shot, and they fell upon a piece of ice: but, as we were rowing round it, in search of a convenient spot to ascend, the ship again became in a state of uproar, and the shout of "a fall!" was vociferated by all on board. The chase of the birds was consequently abandoned for a nobler pursuit, and our boat, with the other four, was rowed to the one attached to the fish, which was upwards of two miles distant, and which, besides its jack flying, had two oars elevated as signals that early assistance was required; not long after a third oar was raised to evince that the demand for aid was pressing. Never was a boat-race better contested, and never was greater exertion made by men to reach the goal. On our passage, the straight line of direction was interrupted by several large flat pieces of ice, some of them bearing hummocks mountain high. At length, when within a quarter of a mile, was presented to our view this "great Leviathan of old," incessantly rising to blow, and at times rearing itself in the air, in all the attitudes characteristic of rage, displaying to man that, were it sensible of its power and strength, the destruction of those who dared to approach it could not fail to be inevitable. At one instant, its immense head was greatly elevated, and a cloud of fume issued from its organs of respiration; it then raised its mountain-back, bristling with the goading harpoon, which it endeavoured to displace by various contortions of its body; finally throwing itself into a perpendicular posture, with its head downward, and its monstrous tail lifted to a surprising height, it made the lobes crack by the effort with which they were whirled in every direction, and dashed them upon the surface with a violence, that could not have failed to annihilate whatever had opposed its force.

On receiving a harpoon from a boat near us, the whale descended perpendicularly with prodigious velocity; but, on its returning to the surface, we could distinguish at a great depth, that it was coming in a direction towards the spot we had taken. Our undaunted harpooner thus cheered the crew " give way, my lads, to pull upon her back ; never mind yourselves." I was placed at the stern of the boat, which was very narrow, and was standing upon some loose ropes. The whale arose with all the grandeur imaginable, making a column of water appear to boil around it, by its great bulk, and rapidity of ascent, at a boat's length from us. On raising its monstrous head, and ejecting a loud and powerful blast, I fired a charge of small shot into it, as the only means in my power to contribute towards securing the prize. At the same time, the harpooner plunged his weapon up to the socket in its back, which caused the fish to make a most convulsive exertion to disengage itself, driving the boat with such extraordinary force against a piece of flat ice, that it was astonishing it was not dashed to pieces. From the insecure situation in which I was standing, having scarcely taken the gun from my shoulder, I was thrown by the effect of the concussion over the boat-steerer's oar, and fell upon the ice, but this fortunately being covered with snow, I received no injury. Instantly recovering myself, I attempted to regain the boat, but the fish had drawn it out of reach, so that I was left to make my observations, the whale being within a few yards of me. The agony the poor animal now appeared to be suffering, would, on any other occasion, have excited sentiments of unmixed compassion; in the present instance the spectacle was rendered awfully grand by the astonishing exertions made by the fish with its fins and tail, to destroy its assailants. The other boats having come up, the crews actively applied lances to reach the vitals of the fish, and I imagine they speedily effected their object; for, in discharging the air from the blow-holes, it gave early indication of exhaustion, by a mixture of blood with the breath. The bustle of the combat—the confusion of voices—the struggle of departing life tinging the air with red—the surrounding sea turned to an ocean of blood—and, at the moment, when the last breath was observed to escape, three hearty cheers from the crews of the boats, to welcome the event,—all together presented a picture beyond the power of description. As soon as the bustle was over, a boat came for me, and the fish being secured by the tail, and the fins tied across the belly, it was, by the united efforts of every boat, rowed to the ship; this was a most cheerful part of the business, being accompanied with a merry song by all the men: on reaching the ship, the fish was placed along-side for the operation of flincing. After waiting this process, in anxious expectation that, by examining the contents of its stomach, I should be able to ascertain the quality of its food, and also to make many other important discoveries of the economy of nature in the structure of the whale, I regretted to find that, from its immense weight, the body of the fish sunk so much below the surface of the water, as totally to prevent an inspection. It was impossible to look upon this immense animal, and to think of the scene which I had just witnessed, without remembering a passage from *Crabbe's Tales of the Hall*, descriptive of the same circumstances.

> I sought the men returned from regions cold,
> The frozen straits where icy mountains roll'd,
> Some I could win, to tell me serious tales
> Of boats uplifted by enormous whales:
> Or, when harpooned, how swiftly through the sea
> The wounded monsters with the cordage flee;
> Yet some uneasy thought assailed me then,
> The monsters warred not with, nor wounded, men:
> The smaller fry we take with scales and fins,
> Who gasp and die, this adds not to our sins:
> But so much blood, warm life, and frames so large,
> To strike, to murder—seemed a heavy charge.

May 26. Several unicorns were playing not far from the ship; I went in pursuit, but the extreme brightness of the day, prevented my getting near them: I, however, shot upwards of twenty of the *Procellaria glacialis*, (LINN.,) or *Fulmar's Peteril*. These birds were met with soon after we had left England, and in the arctic circle they abound: they keep chiefly in the high seas, feeding on dead whales, or any other fleshy substance, that floats on the surface; they will also pick the fat from the backs of the living whales, especially of the wounded, following the bloody track, by hundreds, to watch their rising. The bill of these birds is very strong, yellow, and much turned at the point, resembling that of a hawk; they vary much in their general plumage and in size somewhat exceed the common gull. I saw some, having their breast and neck perfectly white, while others were entirely brown: from the ferociousness of the former, their fighting with each other, and from their never attacking those of dark plumage, I judged them to be the males, and the latter the females. Their flight resembles a running on the surface of the water, whence they are called by the Norwegians, Havhest, or Sea-horse; and, Storm-fugt, or Storm-fowl, as being supposed to presage tempests; the Dutch call them Mallmache, or the foolish-fly, from their number and their stupidity. They seldom come to the land, except when they lose their way in the mists, which are so frequent on the coast of Greenland; and they breed in the broken rocks about Disco, remote from the main land. In the afternoon, I shot one of those very shy birds, the *Larus Glaucus*, (LINN.,) called by the Dutch, Burgermeister, from its being the master of all other sea-fowls within the arctic regions. It is an elegant bird, builds its nest on high cliffs, and preys on cetaceous fishes and small birds; it seldom strays far from the land, but is almost continually on the wing, and generally without any associate. Its bill is yellow, with an orange-coloured spot near the end; head and lower part of the body white; back and wings of a fine hoary grey; primaries darkest, and tipped with white; legs of a pale cadaverous hue; length, from the bill to the tail, twenty-eight inches; extent of wing, five feet; its cry is remarkably harsh, and so loud, as distinctly to be heard when the bird is not to be seen.

May 27. Early this morning, (Sunday,) the officer of the watch reported to the captain, that a very large whale was lying on the surface of the water, near the ship, and asked permission to lower a boat and attack it, but was refused; two or three hours afterwards, on its rising again, the officer returned, making the same application, urged by the crew, who had actually carried one of the harpooners by force into the boat, and were preparing to lower it down; but the same denial was not only peremptorily made, but an order issued that the fullest reverence to the day must be observed. Thus did the Sabbath bring with it the charms of peace, while our Christian captain taught the lessons of gentleness and forbearance to his crew. In the morning service he read to them a most appropriate and impressive sermon from the twentieth chapter of Exodus, and the eighth verse: "Remember the Sabbath-day, to keep it holy." This religious lecture was evidently felt by his hearers, and their hearts were not only softened, but reconciled to a temporary respite from the work of violence.

May 28. Soon after breakfast, Captain Scoresby, from the mast-head, caught a glimpse of a whale descending, and instantly ordered a boat to be sent in pursuit; as the boat approached the place pointed out, it rose, and lay upon the water, as if in a torpid state, until it received the fatal harpoon; on the call of " a fall!" five other boats were despatched, and the fish soon rose again in water free from ice, where it exhibited less energy than is usual in such cases; as the ship was brought to the scene of action, we had an opportunity of distinguishing all that passed. The boats having approached it, and applying their missiles of destruction, it soon gave evident signs of exhaustion, making but one feeble struggle to disengage itself from its enemies; in doing which, it warned the boats to keep at a safe distance, while it rolled about in the agonies of death, until it had lost its strength, when the lances terminated its existence. It was a very large fish, in many parts striped, and marked with large spots of the purest white. The edges of the fins and tail were diversified, and beneath it was much marked with the same colour; its nose and lower jaw were yellow, an evident symptom of great age; and probably its easy capture may be attributed to the decay of nature, as manifested in its feeble resistance and early exhaustion. It was towed to the ship for flincing, when nothing was particularly observable, but that its skin was thinner, its blubber of a higher colour than usual, and the reticulated cells in which the oil is contained, much thicker and tougher, and consequently retaining less oil than is found in a full-grown proper-aged fish. The length of its laminæ was twelve feet eleven inches and a quarter, a size very rarely seen; the extreme length of the fish, fifty-two feet; and the extent of the tail, twenty-one feet.

Among the subjects of natural history found in these regions, is the *Oniscus ceti*, vulgarly called the whale-louse. We saw several of these animals upon the body and jaws of this whale; they are about the size of a very small crab, and covered with remarkably hard scales, the head being similar to that of the *Pediculus humanus*, with four horns, two of which serve as feelers; the other two are hard, curved, and serve as clinches, to fix the animals to the subject which they attack: underneath the chest they have two carvers, like scythes, with which they collect their food; and behind these are four feet that serve the purpose of oars; they have six other clinches behind, with which they rivet themselves so fast to the whale, that they cannot be disengaged, but by cutting out the part to which they are affixed: they are joined in the back similarly to those of the lobster, and the tail covers them like a shield.

May 29. The waste of the ship being almost filled with the blubber, thrown in at the flincing of the three whales which we had now taken, the uncommon fineness of the day was an inducement to proceed to the business of paring and barrelling it, which is termed "*making off*:" for this purpose, the ship was moored to a piece of ice, when, the water being exceedingly clear, we had an opportunity of estimating its depth below the surface. On inquiring of Captain Scoresby, what proportional difference there was between the height of floating ice above the water, and its depth below, he observed, that the irregularities of its shape above the surface prevented the formation of any certain rule to determine this point, but that, usually, the depth of ice below the water was to its height above the surface, as eight, or nine, to one; now, as the average height of the piece to which we were moored, was about six feet, the mass might fairly be considered as a solid body of fifty feet in thickness.

The making off now commenced: the quadrilateral pieces of blubber being brought upon deck, and the skin pared off, they were thrown into a hopper, and cut into small pieces by a very ingenious and simple machine, which allowed them to drop into a canvass tube, called a "*lull-bag*," and from thence into a tub in the hold. The blubber was afterwards put into casks previously arranged for its conveyance to England. Captain Scoresby and myself had some excellent shooting of Burgomasters, *Larus eburneus*, Linn., or snow-birds, and *Fulmar's Peteril*. The bill of the Larus eburneus is of a deep lead colour; the edges and tips yellowish; it is two inches in length from the angle of the mouth; the orbits of the eyes are red; the index brown; the legs and feet black; the whole plumage of the purest white; the length of the bird nineteen inches; its extent of wing forty-one inches. An incredible number of the *Promilarica glaucus*, surrounded the ship during the making off; these carnivorous birds, as before observed, feed on blubber or any oily substance that they discover floating on the water.; a piece being thrown overboard, they swarmed around it, and so intent were they on their prey, that they suffered themselves to be knocked down, rather than relinquish it; and, in flying to partake of this rich banquet, several came so near to the ship as to be struck with the boat-hook.

May 30. The making off not being finished, the ship remained moored, and I shot several birds, among which were three of the *Larus Rissa*, (LINN.,) or Kittywakes. This is the most elegant of the class of gulls, and particularly graceful in its flight; its bill is of a beautiful lemon yellow; orbits of the eye and inside of the mouth bright red; index straw colour; legs livid colour; top of the head, nape, back, and wings, of a fine ash colour; tips of the wings and coverts black; and the rest of the bird white. This gull undergoes three alterations of colour: in the first stage of its life, the coverts of its wings have dark brown feathers; in the second stage, similar dark brown feathers extend over its back, and the tips of its wings are also tinged with the same colour; and in the last, it derives all the character peculiar to the *Larus rissa*; the vulgar name of Kittywake is doubtless derived from the cry of the bird, which sounds exactly as if it said "Kitty's awake." I should have observed, that I this day procured specimens of the three distinct gradations in the change of colour which I have noticed.

May 31. The crew having recovered from their fatigue, and the ship being well cleansed from the grease and filth that attended the unpleasant operation of making off, we unmoored from the ice at ten o'clock, and sailed to the southward, traversing a vast space of ocean, the face of which was often studded with ice of varied forms, and of different extent from a rood to several acres in surface. Often did the ship, under full sail, pass through openings scarcely wider than itself, and frequently not only was the horizon obscured in a mist, but the ship became wrapt in a vapour so dense, as to render our situation extremely perilous among the numerous obstacles that lay in our way. After several fruitless attempts to find a passage from the ice, we at length succeeded, again entered the open sea, and, not having seen a whale for several days, steered to the northward, in hopes of further and better success.

June 4. We sailed by the side of a long piece of ice, called a sea-stream; it lay in the direction of north-east and south-west, often varying from that line in different meanderings, yet keeping its contiguity; from the mast-head the eye was unable to determine its extent, but, from what passed under my observation, it might fairly be presumed to be at least fifty miles; it varied in breadth from one hundred yards to several miles. This curious phenomenon is not generally found, and the imagination is at a loss to conceive by what agency the detached pieces, of which it is composed, are connected, and how they retain their position. Captain Scoresby, whose discerning eye never suffered an advantage to be lost, on observing a small opening, scarcely exceeding the breadth of the ship, availed himself of it, and we passed through it; we had not proceeded more than a hundred yards beyond the opening, when it closed; while passing I examined it with attention, to discover, if possible, the manner of its connexion, and the cause of its temporary chasm, and subsequent attraction; but any attempt to offer an explanation on this curious subject must be built upon mere conjecture.

June 6. The day being perfectly calm, and the sun shining in its brightest splendour, I observed, for the first time in these regions, the ice yielding to its influence, and every mass giving dazzling proofs of its genial warmth. Captain Scoresby and myself, after taking a shooting cruise, went on board the Trafalgar of Hull, commanded by Captain Lloyd, who had, on a previous voyage to Greenland, sailed in the Baffin as first mate, and had been distinguished as a most skilful and active whale-fisher. Our conversation was upon harpoon-guns, and I was gratified in finding that he was fully sensible of the important advantages to be derived from them; in confirmation of his impression of their utility, he informed us that he kept a gun always ready in one of his boats. Perceiving that he was so partial to the harpoon-gun, as to use it under his own personal superintendence, and also that he had formed a very favourable opinion of my plan, I re-

G

quested him to take the charge of one of my guns, supplying him with ammunition, harpoons, and also shells and carcases, to be tried upon such active and resolute whales, as were dangerous to approach, and difficult to conquer.

June 7. At two o'clock in the morning we met with the Enterprise of Lynn, Captain Sanderson. As that officer had interested himself deeply in my inventions, and had given me much useful information on the whale-fishery, I went on board his ship, and requested him to take the charge of one of my hand-harpoons, to which he readily acceded, promising to give it the fullest trial whenever an opportunity should offer. On leaving the Enterprise, we entered a region of ice, consisting of pieces of great magnitude, different from any I had hitherto seen. A very intelligent man, the captain of a Bremen ship, came on board, and requested to be instructed in my method of saving persons from shipwreck. To him I gave one of my lectures, detailing and illustrating the subject, for which he expressed himself greatly obliged, and seemed to anticipate considerable pleasure in disseminating its contents in his own country.

Nothing could exceed the interesting variety which this day's sailing presented. The pieces of ice varied in form and size, and as we passed through the intricacies between them, the greatest dexterity was requisite, to catch the favourable moment at which they offered a passage; and the utmost exertion became necessary to get beyond their reach, lest,

CLOSE PACKED ICE.

London. Pub by G. & W.B. Whittaker Ave Maria Lane.

by closing again, they should crush us to pieces. For the first time during this voyage, the Baffin had her progress arrested ; not, however, for more than an hour and a half, but our situation, while that period lasted, was extremely critical, and prodigious exertions were used by the crew to free us from our icy prison. About seven o'clock in the evening, on entering a large bay, nearly surrounded by *close-packed** ice, several whales were seen at different parts, near its verge ; this gave to us all a joy, not easily described. Boats were instantly sent to the different stations appointed for them, there to wait for the re-appearance of a whale ; one of the boats, and also the gun-boat in which I was, (the harpooner having recovered from his illness) were ordered to as favourable a spot as could be selected, and from which whales had just retired : it was the point of two contiguous small bays, commanding a good view into each of them ; here we remained perfectly still, and narrowly watching for the appearance of our destined prey. This was to me a period of anxiety and expectation, that it would be impossible to describe. We had not been here long, when some whales were seen to rise at the opposite side of the bay, and two boats made *a start*, (that is, they rowed with the greatest rapidity) towards them ; harpoons were thrown without success, and whether these

---

* A body of drift-ice of such magnitude, that its extent is not discernible ; and the pieces of which, though near each other, do not generally touch.

fish gave the alarm to others, it is impossible to say, but they were seen swimming in all directions, and I witnessed several other harpoons thrown ineffectually at distances, at which, *I would have warranted certain destruction to every one of the fish from my gun*, for not any of them exceeded ten yards; but, strange to tell, not a whale came near the boat in which I was, though we changed our situation with every favourable prospect: this being the first time since his recovery that the harpooner appointed to the gun-boat attended, I watched him to ascertain whether he was also prejudiced against my plan; and I regret to say, that his conduct was most unsatisfactory. Finding, also, that I must conform to the instructions said to be given to him, of having a hand-harpoon fastened to my line, in readiness to apply in case of a failure, I considered this want of confidence not only so unnecessary, but likewise so unjust, until a failure had actually taken place, that I became quite indifferent about using the gun, and particularly, as *a most disgraceful trick had been employed to defeat its going off*. I therefore determined not to take further interest in proving its decided advantage, but to use it in amusing myself; and wished them better success than had hitherto attended their taking fish by the hand-harpoon. During our absence from the ship, we had one of the prettiest chases possible, for keeping up continued expectation; this was in pursuing a whale, by the wake, or eddy of water, caused by its swimming not far below the surface; the rapidity of its movements kept our boat's crew in the utmost exertion, for upwards of two miles: but, it had most probably been frightened by some other boat, for, without rising, or allowing us to see it, it swam to a good retreat under a floe of ice. At twelve o'clock, the boats were recalled by a signal; when it was admitted that, had they been provided with gun-harpoons, at least four or five fish would have been captured, as the number of whales that had been seen was unusually great. Captain Scoresby, from the masthead, counted thirty-two different fish.

June 8. Scarcely had I been an hour in bed, when I heard the uproar usual on striking a whale; I arose, and soon saw it killed, and a *sucker* brought on board. It would be wise, if the fishers agreed among themselves, not to take whales of so small a size, as, if not altogether unprofitable, they scarcely pay the incidental expenses; but, such general forbearance would probably never be consented to, since most masters of ships pride themselves on the number of fish which they take without reference to their size. Two whales were afterwards seen, and boats despatched after them, but a thick fall of snow came on, and prevented our watching their movements. Captain Scoresby, from the mast-head, informed me that one of the largest walruses he had ever seen, was upon a piece of ice not far from the ship; a boat was instantly lowered for me, and, loading my gun with ball, we went in pursuit; but unfortunately it heard us approach, looked at us in the manner here represented and plunged into the water; I fired, and though at too great a distance to kill, yet the shot certainly hit it, for it went bleeding to the edge of the water, as we saw by the blood which it left on the snow.

The walrus has been known to attain the length of eighteen feet, and the girth of twelve or thirteen. The head of this hideous animal is small, and so connected to the neck, that it appears to be a continuation of it; the eyes are small, and sunk into the head; the lips fat, and beset with long stout bristles; the skin, which is about an inch thick, hangs in folds or wrinkles, particularly about the neck, and is covered with short bristly hair, of a dirty yellow or greenish colour; the legs are short, and the feet are like those of a seal. Walruses are very numerous about Spitzbergen, and are sometimes seen collected in groups, on pieces of floating ice, where they lie huddled together grunting like swine, or rolling about; the whole group sometimes fall asleep, with the exception of one who is appointed to watch; he however frequently doses, and at such times they may be easily approached and killed. The mothers invariably provide for the safety of their young, in preference to their own, by plunging them into the sea, even when themselves are badly wounded. A striking instance of the affection of a young walrus towards its mother, was related to me: the little animal on seeing its parent killed, became so exasperated, that it singly attacked the boat, and though repeatedly wounded, would not desist, but crawled upon the ice after the men, till a lance entered its heart, and terminated its existence.

We now rowed in pursuit of a whale that came up to blow, but after it had gracefully waved its majestic tail, it descended before we were near enough to commence a combat; in hopes of its return, we waited about half an hour near a large piece of ice, from under which two other whales made their appearance, but were too shy to let us approach them. After rowing about for some time, we returned to the ship; when another whale being seen, I went in the boat, in which I had been during the morning, as I was determined neither to take my harpoon-gun, nor to go with the man appointed to the gun-boat. We were ordered to proceed beyond a point of ice, belonging to an extensive field upwards of a mile from the ship: as we were going to our destination, we heard the blast of a whale among the ice; presently it was repeated, and about one hundred and fifty yards from us, we saw the vapour of its breathing issue from a small opening in the ice; like smoke from a chimney, it rose until it mingled with, and was lost in the atmosphere, and, immediately afterwards, we beheld the object of our pursuit. Never even in my youth, when numbered among the keenest of sportsmen, did I feel so much delight at the sight of game as on this occasion. The boat was instantly brought to the edge of the ice, and the harpooner, being armed with his weapon while the boat's crew and myself conveyed line, we all ran to the spot where the fish was lying; it appeared much above the surface of the water, and had a harpoon already attached to it; our harpooner soon drove his weapon into its mountain back, when the fish instantly went under the ice, and ran out two lines, with a velocity truly astonishing, for its friction in passing round the bollard enveloped us in smoke. The fish rose to breath in a small opening, about half a mile distant; and the contrast of its black arched back, rising above the surface of ice, which was covered with the purest white, had a most extraordinary appearance. The crew of a boat stationed in a bight where we had left the ship, pursuing a similar plan, carried with them a harpoon and lines, and soon struck it again, but it swam off with equal rapidity, until it rose about a quarter of a mile from us. Though I now hastened with two lances towards the spot, it went down tail foremost before I arrived, and therefore I returned to the boat, and found that it had not only run out our complement of six lines, but also three others belonging to a boat that had been sent to our assistance. I now observed the boat from which the second harpoon had been struck, moving rapidly along the ice, over large hummocks, while its crew were exerting their utmost strength to impede its progress. From the commencement of the attack, we had used our best endeavours to check the career of this resolute fish, but human efforts were for the present unable to control its power. Determined, however, not to give more line, we put over the stern a heavy grapnel and long tow-line, to which every man held on with his utmost strength, while I, having got into the boat to travel in this unusual manner, was drawn with great speed to the place where the whale was first struck; here, to prevent the boat being taken under the ice, more line was given, but to no great extent. Fortunately, the whale quitted the ice, and came up in open water; when we had soon the pleasure of seeing a jack displayed from another of the boats to announce that a third harpoon had struck the prey. About a quarter of an hour after this, we heard the welcome shout which follows the death of a fish.

Our boat's crew being engaged in pulling in the line, I had an opportunity of exploring part of this extensive plain of ice which was immeasurable to the eye. This dreary waste was wholly composed of newly-created ice, and, rising from the surface of the ocean, was in many places perfectly flat, while in others, it was covered with hillocks, especially on the north side, where the massive pieces that had been forced upon it by the violence of storms, were generally in an upright position, so that the snow could not lodge upon the summits. Several yawning chasms that I had passed over in the ardour of the chase, I examined on my return; and found the ice to vary in thickness from three feet to a thin stratum that would have been dangerous to pass over. Traces of bears, whose footsteps were very large, were observable on its surface. The rich tint of blue that filled the shades, gave a beautiful variety to this immense tract of whiteness. I can conceive nothing similar to it, unless it should be an unbounded plain covered with fragments of rock, and encased in snow.

The lines, after three hours' labour, having been hauled in and coiled up, we returned to the ship, where, perhaps, the most beautiful whale ever beheld, was lying, with its belly uppermost, ready for flincing. No admirer of black cattle ever saw in a favourite breed, marks more pleasing to the eye, better in their arrangement, or stronger contrasts of the purest black and white, than were exhibited on this fish. I now learned some interesting particulars of this extraordinary whale; besides fifteen lines of two hundred and forty yards each, which it had taken from our own boats, it had fast to it, six similar lines, a harpoon, and a boat belonging to the Trafalgar. For the purpose of affording an idea of the animal's strength, I may mention, that it carried five thousand and forty yards of rope, weighing upwards of a ton and a half, without any calculation being made of the resistance given by the sunken boat, by the boats over the snow, and by fifteen men.

The boats having all returned, and the crews being ready for flincing, the ship was moored to leeward of the field of ice, and the harpooners, with their cutting-knives and blubber-spades, were ready to commence the operation; but the flincing was soon stopped by the rising of another whale about a mile from us. After resting upon the surface for a few minutes, it disappeared in the manner usual when not disturbed, by slowly elevating its back, with a graceful movement of the tail. The boat sent in pursuit, took its station against a piece of flat ice, where it had not remained long, before the fish again rose near a lofty hummock connected with the ice to which the ship was moored; the sea being perfectly smooth, much address was requisite, and the boat was most skilfully sculled upon its back, into which a harpoon was deeply driven; the agitation instantly produced on the still water, was astonishing; and the sudden darting down of the fish, placed the harpooner in considerable danger of being thrown overboard, by the boat's heeling from the action of the tail; and the boat-steerer had also great difficulty in keeping his balance. Instantly, with great velocity, the whale dived under the ice, and ran out six lines in a very short time; a boat with a fresh supply arrived, their lines were united to the others, and the whale continued without the slightest intermission to run out four of these. The direction of its course being observed by Captain Scoresby, he despatched boats round the point, and so judiciously did he arrange their situation in a bight about a mile and a half distant, that on the fish rising to breathe, it received a second harpoon, of which we were informed by the welcome signal of the jack; soon after a similar signal was raised of a third harpoon being fast; the fish having been perfectly exhausted, it now gave little trouble, and presently we heard the grateful sound of three cheers to announce its capture. The five boats towed it to the side of the ship, when I left the operation of flincing for the enjoyment of some rest, having had only four hours during the last forty-eight, and endured more anxiety, exertion, and fatigue, than I had undergone for many years. The bone of one of the whales was reported to measure ten feet eleven inches, and of the other ten feet seven inches in length; they were both males.

June 9. The ship being cleaned, and the men having enjoyed some rest, we unmoored. As the wind began to blow, and the adjoining ice threatened to incommode us, we sailed to the westward, and, on coming to a field of ice, Captain Scoresby urged me to go aloft with him, and examine its extent; I complied, and having ascended with some difficulty, was most richly repaid, for this continent of ice was unlike any thing that I had ever before seen; it was composed of a series of rugged hills varying in size, and rising in sharp

angles, some of which were forty feet high; its front was a bluff and craggy barrier of several feet in height, from which it was evident that large masses had been separated. In parts of this line, bays of considerable depth had been formed, gradually sloping from the margin of the sea to the higher termination. The wind increasing, and the ice indicating a general movement, we sailed to a considerable distance and lay to.

June 11. A gale coming on, we kept under the lee of the ice-field, which not only screened us from its fury, but kept us undisturbed by the swell of the sea, so that the ship to my great comfort lay in a state of comparative rest. I had now leisure to examine with attention the formation of that curious phenomenon, a field of ice, which exhibited proofs of its receiving annual accumulations by distinct tiers or layers, formed most probably by the melted snow of preceding winters. Several very heavy floes were seen drifting past us at a great rate, and I could not help imagining, with feelings of horror, the possibility of our being caught between two of them and encountering the inevitable destruction, that from their immense pressure must necessarily follow.

June 12. A fog with drifting snow, that, on minute investigation, displayed a beautiful specimen of regular hexagonal form, rendered the day unfavourable for fishing; and therefore a mass of ice, to which it would be safe to moor, was anxiously looked for; after much search, a piece in a favourable position was selected for the purpose. It may be proper to remark, that the greatest observation and most strict attention are requisite in mooring a ship against a floe of ice, in a situation where other immense masses are in motion; for I noticed that large bodies of ice do not move directly to leeward, as would naturally be supposed, but, like a ship, form a curvature, greater or less, according to their elongated form. Several ships were now in company; some pursuing their avocation, others moored like ourselves to the ice, and one of them to an iceberg. The disagreeable process of making off the three whales last caught, was now performed; this being finished, and the ship cleaned, we unmoored at three o'clock, and sailed again in search of whales. One, of an immense size, rose not far from us, but very near the Trafalgar, and was struck by a harpooner from that ship, who actually ran his boat upon the back of the fish. The wind was blowing very hard, and the whale, in going down, nearly upset the boat, by raising it on its tail; it very quickly ran out all the lines, and went under a field of ice; when from the harpoon not retaining its hold, the fish was lost. This method of close approach to a whale is common in the fishing when circumstances will allow, as it prevents the fish, from the situation of his eyes, from perceiving the meditated design; it is nevertheless a service of considerable hazard, and was, in this instance, of extraordinary peril: boats are thus often lifted out of the water; and, I have been assured, have in some instances, been raised so high above the surface, as to throw out all the crew, and to expose both men and boats to one common destruction of which, the following circumstance is related by Captain Scoresby. " In one of my earliest voyages to the whale fishery, a harpooner of our ship struck a whale, when, in descending, it projected the boat and all its crew to the height of some yards in the air."

June 13. The ship was kept close under the lee of a field of ice, where, though the wind was blowing a gale, we lay in smooth water, and towards the evening saw a whale, fast travelling to the southward, which neither our boats nor those of other vessels could prevent.

June 14. The gale continued with increased fury all the day, so that the whole fleet of vessels, either got under close-reefed topsails to leeward of the field of ice, or moored to it. This apparent continent, it is presumed, forms one uninterrupted sheet of ice, extending to the western land upwards of one hundred miles: and, with the exception of that part next the ocean, where there are occasional openings, not a fissure was observable in it. Two vessels, we could perceive, were in a perilous situation, but at that period no assistance could be rendered them; they were beset by ice, and must remain imprisoned, till liberated by the separation of the floes, either from the influence of the wind, or from some other favourable contingency. The captains of two Greenland ships came on board and dined; one of them was a most intelligent, experienced, and successful whale-fisher, from the port of Hull, who gave me much information on the subject of his avocation: the other was the commander of a ship from a Scottish port. The Caledonian had not been fortunate during this voyage; and, like many impatient characters, could not bear, with christian fortitude, reverses from which he conceived that his experience and perseverance should have exempted him. The wind continued to blow from the north with extreme violence, and we sailed towards the east.

June 15. A bright sun, whose shining beams ever give delight, induced me to rise early, and the pleasing sight of a rich blue sky welcomed me on deck. The ship appeared to be in a large basin, with twenty other vessels, surrounded by a horizon that was covered with ice; part of this was a continuation of the field near which we had kept during the last two days; the other part was formed of immense pieces connected with it. A whale having been seen to retire under the ice, the boats from many ships were sent in pursuit, and kept under the ridge of the ice watching for its reappearance; the oddity of the scene was so great, that I could not help comparing the boats to cats watching at the holes of mice, in readiness to seize their prey, as soon as they should have the hardihood to venture from their places of security.

The wind having abated during the night, we sailed the whole of this day by the side of the ice, until, towards evening, the breeze changing to the south, we kept under the lee of this noble breakwater, and ran to the opposite side which had afforded us shelter yesterday; this gave us an opportunity of estimating its extent, which was upwards of twenty miles north and south, and more than ten miles east and west. The ship's run this day was truly interesting; for, on looking forward, a person, unaccustomed to the navigation of these seas, would have considered it impossible for a vessel in a strong wind, to sail through an ocean encumbered by huge masses of ice in every direction. At eight o'clock, a thick fog came on; and a heavy fall of snow, accompanied with a gale of wind, closed the day.

June 16. During the night the wind suddenly abated to a perfect calm, but this did not lull Captain Scoresby into security, nor induce him to put more sail upon the ship, as the faithful herald of the movements of the elements (the barometer) foretold an impending storm; he, consequently, kept the ship under close-reefed topsails, though every other vessel in company increased the number of their sails. In an instant, the wind commenced blowing with fury, and in a contrary direction to the last gale, causing the ice which before had been a friendly shelter, now to become a dangerous foe. The violence of the gale making it hazardous to beat through a sea thickly strewed with heavy pieces of ice, to regain the comfortable shelter we

H

experienced yesterday, it was therefore deemed expedient to run into open water for security. Scarcely did I experience, during the voyage, a more unpleasant night; a continued fall of snow rendered the cold intense. The violence of the gale often laid the vessel on her "beam ends;" and the heavy blows that she received from the ice, the effect of which I can only compare to the shock sustained by a ship in striking against sunken rocks, would have occasioned me the most serious apprehensions for our safety, if I had not become habituated to the incidents of an arctic voyage.

June 18. Having lay to the greater part of yesterday, for the purpose of attending to the duties of the Sabbath, and the wind this morning abating to a gentle breeze from the north, we sailed towards the body of western ice. The seamanship displayed during this day, in making judicious boards, to weather points that occurred in our course through a long, strait, and treacherous opening in the ice, was beyond all praise. It is impossible to conceive any thing more interesting than the intricacies of the passage between floes of various sizes, many of which had evidently been broken from fields during the late gales. The sun dazzled my eyes by its glow upon the snow-clad ice, and the temperature of the thermometer became reduced to thirty-five degrees.

The effect of this powerful exhalation soon began to indicate what might be expected; a thick fog-bank was seen rising from the horizon; and scarcely had we accomplished our passage into a fine space of water, when a most dense fog enveloped us.

June 19. The density of the fog prevented our seeing objects scarcely a ship's length from us, and consequently the vessel was run against several pieces of ice during the night; in the morning, the wind changed to the south-west, and blew a hurricane all the day, during which we had most fearful sailing between floes that were in rapid motion, but which were passed with great adroitness. As the wind abated, the fog became more dense, and our companion, the Trafalgar, like ourselves, was encompassed by an impenetrable barrier of ice, which the gale had collected. Finding that there was no opening to proceed, and that the one through which we had come was closed, our situation was considered perilous, and the apprehension of being beset was entertained by every one conversant with the nature of the ice. The only consolation was, that the wind having ceased, there were hopes of our being enabled to cut a dock in a floe, large enough to receive the ship; this would be less dangerous than being forced between a stationary field, and a floe driven by the impulse of the elements, with a fury against which no human ingenuity could avail in preventing the inevitable destruction that must ensue. Happily we were not reduced to the extremity which we had so much reason to dread.

That some opinion may be formed of the dangers

arising from the drifting of heavy ice, I shall refer to Captain Scoresby's account of the tremendous concussion of fields. He observes that the occasional rapid motion of ice fields, attended with the destructive effects, which are produced on any opposing substance, exhibits one of the most striking, and, at the same time, one of the most terrific sights, which Greenland produces. These bodies not unfrequently acquire a rotary motion, by which their circumference attains a velocity of several miles an hour. If a field, thus in motion, comes in contact with another at rest, or more especially in a contrary direction of movement, the shock is dreadful. Some faint idea may, indeed, be conceived of the consequences which must ensue, when a body of more than ten thousand millions of tons in weight* encounters resistance to its motion. The weaker field is crushed to atoms, with an awful noise; sometimes the destruction is mutual; pieces of huge dimensions, are not unfrequently piled to the height of twenty or thirty feet upon the top, whilst, doubtless, a proportionate quantity is depressed beneath. These stupendous effects, when viewed in safety, exhibit a picture sublimely grand; but where there is danger of being over-

* Captain Scoresby estimates that a field containing thirty nautical square miles in surface, with a thickness of thirteen feet, would weigh more than is here mentioned, allowing it to displace the water in which it floats to the depth of eleven feet. The weight would appear to be 10,182,857,142 tons, nearly in the proportion of a cubic foot of sea water to sixty-four pounds.

whelmed, terror and dismay must be the predominant feelings. The whale-fishers at all times require unremitting vigilance to ensure their safety, but scarcely in any situation so much, as when navigating amidst these fields in foggy weather, because their motions then cannot be distinctly observed. It may easily be imagined, that the strongest ships can no more withstand the shock of the contact of two fields, than a sheet of paper can stop a musket-ball. Since the establishment of the whale-fishery, a number of vessels have been thus destroyed; some have been thrown upon the ice, others have been torn completely open, whilst others again have been buried beneath the heaped fragments of ice.

June 20. The shock of a piece of ice striking the bow of the ship a tremendous blow, which made its whole frame to tremble, and the grating of a large mass in passing, as if determined to saw its way through the side of the ship, urged me hastily to the deck. The watch were all in activity; some getting towlines into boats, to tow the ship through a narrow passage, scarcely wider than itself; others on the ice, setting ice-anchors, whilst many were employed at the capstan. After considerable labour, by towing and warping, the ship was removed into more open water, and a breeze springing up, soon freed us from our present difficulties.

The assistance of the boats being no longer required, I availed myself of the opportunity to go in pursuit of three unicorns, but without success. A walrus or sea horse was seen to leeward, but at too great a distance for a boat to be spared. We continued sailing forward in apparent security, with the expectation of a good lead into slacker ice, or probably into open water, when a thick fog suddenly obscured our prospects. Before it cleared away, we found the ice to be rapidly closing, and ultimately we were surrounded by pieces, which, from their magnitude, were frightful to behold; the water being very transparent, they exhibited their awful appendages, termed *tongues**, far protruding below the surface. Every direction that the best judgment could suggest, was given, and the promptest obedience was observed. Two hours were never spent in greater anxiety, activity, and interest, as we sailed over a great space, often between large pieces of ice, until we came into open water, when, the fog returning, the ship lay to. At four o'clock in the afternoon the fog cleared off, but the wind gathered to a gale, and laid the ship on her beam ends almost all the night.

June 21. The wind changed from north to south, and blew with equal violence, putting the ice in motion in every direction. The gales seemed to conspire against the attainment of the interesting object of our pursuit, the WESTERN LAND; for, just as we were preparing to avail ourselves of a favour-

---

* A point of ice projecting nearly horizontally from a part that is under water.

able lead, the further end was observed to be closing, and not only to oppose our progress, but also to point out the necessity of returning as early as possible; repeated were these disappointments during the day, while the wind continued blowing with great fury, compelling us to sail between immense floes, staying round some, and veering round others; in short, we had to steer north, south, and east, to pursue our course. By some it might be considered a day of most fearful sailing, but from its increasing variety, it was to me a time of extraordinary interest. A barrier of impenetrable ice at length arrested our progress, and the ship lay to, in the anxious hope that the gale would interpose in our behalf, and, by abating, enable us to proceed.

Some Liverpool friends having, previous to our sailing, intimated their intention of drinking to Captain Scoresby's good health and mine, precisely at two o'clock this day, as they knew that our time to dine was one o'clock, the chronometer was now consulted, the difference of time between Liverpool and our present station calculated, and the precise moment being ascertained when it was presumed that the clocks of that town would be striking two, our flowing glasses, met with best wishes at our lips, for health and happiness to our absent friends. There is something extremely consolatory and infinitely pleasing to those who are far distant from esteemed relations and friends, to know the very instant when they are interesting themselves in their welfare, and feeling an earnest desire for their health and prosperity.

The ice being observed to open about three o'clock, we had the gratification of again pursuing our western course, through its intricate leads and zig-zag angles, where there was much difficulty in keeping clear from dangerous floes strewed with hummocks; one of these solid masses was at least fifty feet high, thirty feet broad, and twenty feet in thickness; and had doubtless been forced upon the floe when in contact with some other piece. This, with other evidences of the prodigious power of bodies of ice when in motion, I could not behold without feelings of horror, knowing what would be the fate of the Baffin if caught in their clutches. This beautiful day's sailing, which exceeded all that I had hitherto seen, closed with our proceeding as far as the ice would allow; in the evening we were encircled by a dense fog. The altitude of the sun at noon, was 39° 30′ and at midnight 7° 30′.

June 22. The bustle attendant on lowering a boat, called me up from my birth at half past four o'clock; when I arrived upon the deck, I saw the crew of one boat armed with lances and ranged on the borders of the ice, while a second boat was in full chase of an immense bear that had been attacked by the party on the ice, and had kept all its assailants at bay, until it had succeeded in effecting a good retreat into the water. The animal swam so astonishingly fast, that it was at least half

a mile from the ice, before the boat could overtake
it. When this was accomplished, the bear resolutely
faced the boat, and efforts were made to wound it
with lances, but, the thickness of its skin, as the
men stated, was impenetrable to the weapons, though
I cannot help thinking that Bruin's hideous grins,
his loud roar, and his daring attempts to reach the
boat, by intimidating the assailants, kept them at too
great a distance to attack him successfully. After
several conflicts he swam to the ice, where he was
opposed by two men, but whether the lances would
not enter his breast, or whether the men still ap-
prehended the consequences of approaching so formidable an enemy, I know not; but he marched
away uninjured, and I was only astonished that he
did not make a meal of one of the assailants.

After breakfast, we again sailed towards the west.
The difficulties which we had to encounter were
even more numerous than they had hitherto been,
and the nature of our sailing was quite different
from any that had before been exhibited; we had
to work directly against the wind through a passage
or lead, at least three miles in length, and in many
parts not more than a hundred yards wide, with
heavy pieces of ice in the channel. It must be observed that this navigation is totally unlike working
through a narrow passage, with the advantage of a
tide; for here is no such assistance, and every thing
must be attained by nicety in management of the
helm and sail. In no sailing match, even with
numerous vessels in competition, could that skill

for which the Gravesend boats are so justly celebrated, be half so ingeniously displayed, as in keeping clear of the pieces of ice, which now frequently threatened by their overwhelming power to impede the ship's progress. At length we came into more open water, kept our course, and hoped soon to gain our westward destination. We saw with regret that our companion, the Trafalgar, was unable to follow our track; that the ice was in rapid motion; and that in all probability, if that ship was not already beset, she soon would be; but a fog coming on suddenly shut her from our sight. In the course of this day, the ice assumed an entirely new character, consisting principally of pieces about three feet above the surface of the water, without hummocks, quite level, and of all dimensions from a few yards in surface to an extent of many square miles.

We kept our course all night, and in the morning came into a basin perfectly free from floating ice, but surrounded by fields infinitely larger than any we had before seen. It is a remarkable circumstance, that fields of ice are always found with spaces of water on their boundary; whether, this fact has given rise to the hypothesis of a polar basin, I will not presume to say; neither will I offer an opinion on the probability of such a space being formed round the north pole, since so many abler men are undecided upon this interesting question. The inlet into this basin was scarcely a point of the compass in width, resembling the spout of a large jug; we sailed round its impenetrable

June 23.

brim, and, observing this small aperture, made all sail, and succeeded in passing through it just before it closed; we continued our course to the westward, and at four o'clock saw a whale near the edge of the ice. Several boats were sent in pursuit, but returned about eight o'clock without having seen it again. While absent from the ship in this service, I witnessed a sight of much interest to a lover of falconry, in the attack of an arctic gull, (*Larus Parisiticus*, LINN), upon a kittywake. My attention was first directed to it by a screaming at a great height in the air, and at a considerable distance. I observed a sharp conflict for upwards of a quarter of an hour, during which, many bold stoops were made by the gull, and they were as beautifully evaded by the superior aërial movements and dexterity of the kittywake; I never beheld a finer or more active flight at a heron, which it very much resembled. About nine o'clock a whale rose in the midst of our little fleet, which now consisted of five ships; boats being instantly lowered from each, rowed to that part of the ice under which the fish swam, and took their stations against its return. After waiting some time, the old fishing stratagem was put in practice by the boat's crews of two confederate ships: the crew of one of the boats commenced the plan usually adopted on seeing a whale, that is, the harpooner quickly sitting down, takes his oar, and the boat is rowed with the greatest speed, in the expectation that all the rest will follow, leaving the favourable situation open, when boats belonging to the confederate party avail themselves of the absence of the rest, and wait the probable reappearance of the fish. This may be called a *ruse de pêcherie*, and, as I understand, often succeeds. In the present instance, however, it failed, as we liked our stations too well to quit them; though the whale did not shew itself again. The wary fishermen who thus endeavoured to outwit us, belonged to two vessels from Scotland; and although disappointed in their project, they kept a boat near to ours, ready for a start, and one came in front of us, which certainly was unfair, and would tend to alarm a fish, and prevent our success. I intimated my hope, that they would not keep between the fish and our boat, as I had upon the boat's bow a one-pounder loaded with a shell, which I should assuredly throw at the fish. The hint was taken, and the wily Caledonians rowed off.

June 24. Our boat having been recalled at twelve o'clock at night and hoisted up, previous to the commencement of the day, I regretted to see that the same observance of the Sabbath was not attended to by the other ships in company, as they kept their boats ready for service all the day. Our captain very properly ordered his ship away, that the crew might not witness the conduct of those who did not reverence the Sabbath, and lest their example should disturb that orderly deportment which was invariably observed on board this ship on Sunday.

June 25. The Baffin having been withdrawn from the fishing station to the farther part of the basin, the wind changing to the north, set t the ice in motion, and prevented our getting out, though almost all the other ships found a clear lead to the westward; the opening through which they had passed we visited about noon for the same purpose, but found it too hazardous to attempt until four o'clock, when it having indicated a more favourable movement, we again sailed towards it; but the moment we were about to enter, it was observed to be closing very rapidly, and that inevitable destruction would be the consequence of our proceeding. The sails were therefore backed, and the ship lay to, to afford us an opportunity of observing the collision of two heavy bodies of ice; a circumstance fatal to many, and dreaded by all who visit the arctic regions. The meeting was terrifically grand; as soon as the most projecting parts came in contract, they began to rise above the surface in cubical and rhomboidal masses of great magnitude and vast weight, some at least fifty feet long, thirty feet broad, and twenty feet thick; these projections being elevated on the great bed of ice, threw the pressure on parts of yet greater extent, whilst those of higher elevation kept gradually rising and forming an immense bank, as if by some supernatural agency. The whole was calculated to excite the admiration of those who delight in beholding the wonderful works of God.

Being thus shut out, we sailed to the northward, keeping near the margin of the field throughout the day, and intending, if possible, to get round it.

Lat. by observation, 73° 3' N., Long. by chronometer, 9° 30' W.

June 26. The wind changed to the south-west during the night, and blew very hard; in the morning, therefore, every inlet was tried in search of a passage, but in vain; in the course of the day we returned to the part that had closed yesterday, when we found that the fury of the gale had torn from these immense regions of ice, pieces of several acres in extent, and had crumbled others to atoms, leaving the scattered fragments so numerous, that we were obliged to abandon all idea of getting through in that direction; in searching for another opening, the ice became so extremely crowded, that the ship was struck by several heavy pieces, with a violence that made it to recoil with the shock, and which nothing but its extraordinary strength could have withstood. Toward the evening the wind ceased, and became calm with a thick fog, when four ships besides our own were moored to a large piece of ice to prevent their drifting.

June 27. On the fog having cleared away, and the wind blowing strong from the northeast, we again resumed our labour of exploring a passage to the westward. In pursuing this object, nothing could exceed the anxiety of our hopes and fears during the three following days; while those impediments which had so repeatedly defeated our design, continued to render its accomplishment impossible. It was now fully ascertained by our com-

FLOE OF ICE.
London Pub by G.&W.B.Whittaker Ave Maria Lane

panions, as well as by those on board the Baffin, that an infinitely greater accumulation of ice prevailed to the westward, than had been found the preceding season; and some of the experienced seamen were of opinion, that there was at least five times as much as had ever been known. It is impossible for language to describe the interesting, though fearful sailing, which we had witnessed for the last three days, in attempting to get to the west, through the most intricate navigation imaginable, during the whole of which we were opposed by a gale from the north-east, and had the ship generally on its beam ends, from the pressure of sail indispensably necessary to avoid the obstructions that so often occurred. One ship in company had its rudder damaged, and the Baffin suffered in passing through a lead between two lofty pieces of ice, though only in having two boats injured: to hard blows we were now become familiarized, although some were of sufficient violence, as a sailor jocosely expressed it, " to knock the ship's brains out." As we advanced to the westward, our difficulties became lessened, much more open water was found; and the ice consisted of large floes and fields; the former, only measurable by the aid of a glass, the latter beyond the possibility of being ascertained, and only pointed out by the yellow arched tint above the horizon, the reflected mirror of its extraordinary magnitude. It has been generally admitted by all whose avocations have led them to these seas, that more gales prevailed this season than usual, particularly in the present month, which is commonly found to be remarkably fine, calm, open, and clear, with a pleasant temperature, whereas this has been accompanied by repeated gales, with a temperature below that of the freezing point. Our endeavours to penetrate to the westward were so anxiously conducted, as to constitute a perfect voyage of discovery, and no navigator, in the endeavour to explore regions known only by conjecture, could have been kept in more watchful expectation than we were, or have suffered more disappointment than we now experienced.

June 30. A change of weather at length took place, and we were favoured with a most beautiful day. About noon, the wind abated to a gentle breeze, and the sun shone with uncommon lustre, as we entered a large bay, the bottom of which was formed of impenetrable floes of rugged ice, extending from the south-east north about to south-west; thus again was our western progress arrested. Here our squadron of five ships was augmented to twelve, and presented an interesting spectacle as they were all lying-to in the bay. One of our boats was despatched for a load of ice or congealed snow, to be dissolved for the use of the ship's crew, the only means, in this forlorn region, of providing that very necessary article of life; and I availed myself of this opportunity to take a shooting excursion. On my return I went on board the Cato, a ship which had been in company with the Thornton when that vessel was wrecked in May; here I obtained many interesting particulars of the catas-

FIELD OF ICE WITH WATER BLINK.

London, Pub.d by G&W.B. Whittaker, Ave Maria Lane.

trophe; and I learned at the same time, that the Cato, as well as other ships, had nearly shared the same fate, some of them having been lifted up by the ice, several feet above their water line. The destruction of the Thornton in lat. 79° N. was stated to have been progressive for about fifteen minutes, when its sides yielding to the irresistible pressure, the ice formed a junction through the unfortunate wreck. Several other distressing occurrences were enumerated, some where the destruction had been completed within a minute after the ice on either side had come in contact with the vessel.

This day several *Sterna Hirundo*, LINN., or sea-swallow, came flying round and over the ship, but beyond the reach of shot; they appeared extremely elegant birds on the wing, and were singularly attractive from their long tail-feathers which were extendedly forked.

July 1. At four o'clock in the morning, the ice having opened on the north-west side of the bay, all the other ships went out and sailed away to windward, but we remained lying to, until all the duties of the Sabbath had been performed, when we sailed in the same direction; about ten o'clock P. M., a thick fog came on, which made the navigation both difficult and dangerous.

July 2. The weather clearing, we found ourselves in a bay of impenetrable ice, of about six miles in depth, and with no inlet but that through which we came; we therefore lost no time in making a retrograde course. Several unicorns were seen and two boats sent after them: one was struck and brought on board, which was thirteen feet long, and its horn two feet; many of these fish and a large finner whale being seen, I went after them without effect. As I returned I went on board several of the ships which were in company, to submit my plan to them, and to procure any curious subject for the advancement of natural history. In one of them, it being calm, several masters had met to regale themselves (called in Greenland Mullimorking); among them was the master of the Thornton, which in May last, as already mentioned, had been wrecked near Spitzbergen. From this meeting I collected much information, both regarding the fisheries and other circumstances connected with the arctic regions; more particularly as they respected the destruction of vessels by the pressure of the ice. I listened with uncommon attention to the recital of fatal accidents of this nature, and felt deeply for the misfortunes of those who had been sufferers from such calamities; I could not, at the same time, however, refrain from astonishment at the indifference of conduct, and keen enjoyment amidst the hilarity of the meeting, which were evinced by the master of the Thornton. I afterwards visited a ship from Bremen in the hope of collecting some useful information; or at least to make observations on board a foreign ship that might be conducive to my country's benefit: the commander of this ship (the Von Beur) was perfectly familiar with my name, and my reason for visiting this remote part of the world, and gave me every assurance in his power of his satisfaction at seeing me; I found him, as is usual in foreigners, extremely observant, and very inquisitive; he expressed himself particularly anxious to learn my plans for the saving of shipwrecked seamen; and I felt much pleasure in explaining to him the nature, principle, and design of my inventions, assuring him, that warmly as I desired that my country should derive advantage from my labours, I had yet been actuated by the hope, that foreigners would also be enabled to participate in the benefit of them. After I had explained every particular, he shewed me a curious collection which he had made during this voyage of subjects of natural history, and gave me a very fine specimen of a cancer pulex, which he had taken a few days since from the whale he had last caught, it being entangled to the laminæ in the mouth of that fish. He also shewed me a fœtus, taken out of a female narwal, which he had caught in the early part of the voyage; and expressed his regret that it was not in his power to give it to me, because it was designed for the museum at Stockholm, so I contented myself with securing an exact representation of it both in figure and size.

Having taken my leave, I returned to my ship, and on the way shot many arctic birds. On my getting on board, the ship was about to penetrate what had been until a few minutes before an impenetrable barrier of ice, but which was beginning to open to the north-west. This ice which had constituted an immense field, silently opened by a fissure, the previous existence of which had only been suspected by the appearance of a long crack which, winding in different directions and branching into many filaments, extended to a large space of water at least three miles distant; by what agency this separation was effected I will not hazard an opinion. As soon as the opening was sufficiently large to admit the ship by the aid of boats a-head, and the setting of all the sails, we passed along what had been but a short time before a compact body; immense floes of ice were on each side of us extending beyond the reach of the human eye. In this situation it was impossible to preserve my mind from being assailed with horrible apprehensions, of the inevitable result which awaited us, if these boundaries of ice should prove capricious and close around the ship; particularly, as several who were conversant with the navigation of these seas, expressed, in my hearing, their strongest fears of the undertaking, mingled with astonishment at the boldness of the enterprise, and the intrepidity of Captain Scoresby. I am, indeed, still persuaded that nothing but his consummate judgment and superior knowledge in the movements of polar ice, could have succeeded in so daring an attempt. Some of the officers and men near me, having on former occasions escaped only with their lives from ships, the sides of which had been literally squeezed together in a few minutes, exactly in similar situations to the present, made no secret of their apprehensions for the fate of the Baffin. If these fears were not consolatory, I was cheered by a religious thankfulness to God, that we were yet safe and with health to exert ourselves in case of necessity. To strengthen the general opinion which was formed of the undertaking, the four ships which had been in company kept lying to, not daring to follow. Notwithstanding the terrific nature of this navigation, I afterwards learned that Captain Scoresby did not attempt the enterprise until he had satisfied himself that the motion of the ice was favourable to his wishes, and such as with the prudent measures he had adopted, would, by the blessing of God, ensure our safety.

Among the subjects that in these regions are extremely interesting to the philosopher, one of a particular nature occurred this day, in the extraordinary effect and power of refraction. By this phenomenon, the exact representation of vessels at a distance, at which the convexity of the earth would prevent the possibility of their being seen, was presented to us above the horizon in an inverted form. The details of this curious subject will probably be given to the public by the able pen of Captain Scoresby, whose attainments in science so pre-eminently distinguish him; and the result of his observation may therefore be looked for with great interest.

While we were passing between two floes that had formed a neck, and just opened a passage wide enough for the ship to move through, I observed the spiculæ darting with considerable velocity on the surface of the water, in all the pleasing variety of congelation. This excited my particular attention from its occurring in a space, that half an hour before, had been covered by ice, when the contiguous water was perfectly open. The operation here evident, combined with many other proofs I had witnessed to convince me of the fact that seawater does freeze, a circumstance that has been doubted. After a navigation of inconceivable interest, we came by a small inlet into a considerable space of water, surrounded by a field, floes, and seal meadows of ice; where we lay to, not being able to proceed further to the westward in the course which we had been pursuing.

July 4. We moored the ship to a large floe of ice not far distant, and of an extent just to render visible two ships on the opposite side; here the crew were employed in getting fresh water from pools that had been formed by the melting of the snow on the surface of the ice. Three whales were seen, and boats sent after them, but as the fog was dense, and the fish did not re-appear, the boats returned. The usual effects of a calm followed, and brought some of those extreme dangers attendant on the navigation of these seas, by the separation of large bodies of ice at such times. We were thus kept in constant watchfulness, not from imaginary apprehensions, but from the warning of many heavy and extensive pieces, being observed through the mist to threaten to beset us, if not to prove our destruction; some of these masses came with great violence against the ship.

July 7. The fog at length yielded, and became less dense, and we found ourselves not a hundred and fifty yards from the rugged frozen ridge of a field of ice, on which were monstrous masses,—one of them resembling a castle—with a water blink stretching across the horizon. About noon the fog had totally subsided, and from the stillness of the day and the brightness of the sun, the surface of the ocean like a most dazzling mirror, reflected the perfect representation of the four ships in company, every rope in which was distinctly exhibited. Among the different objects so pleasingly reflected, I could not avoid noticing the effect produced from drops of oil exuding from the jaw-bones of a whale which we had killed, and which were suspended at the bows of the ship. When a drop of oil fell from these into the water, the colours produced from refraction were those of the prism in their richest hues; and they continued to change in character and form by the slightest undulation of that great body of water, so that they were rendered as various as the colours of the kaleidoscope and infinitely finer in their tints.

At ten o'clock at night the ice was observed to be in rapid motion, in a course opposed to our proceeding westward; at this time some of the richest clouds I ever beheld, were lining the canopy of heaven: the extraordinary blueness of the water, and its peculiar transparency were astonishingly pleasing. By the optical illusion seen in it, the clouds were here accurately reflected, and appeared to be at a depth equal to their altitude above the surface, while the splendour of their colours was much heightened, and every particle of their woolly foldings distinctly seen. An unicorn was observed near the ship, but the stillness of the weather, and the clearness of the water, prevented the boat which was sent, from getting near it.

July 9. At seven o'clock in the morning, the extremely dense fog which had continued all yesterday cleared, and gave us an opportunity of seeing that a field, floes, and other heavy bodies of ice had been collected, and ranged around us on twenty-six points of the compass; and that only one opening, a very narrow channel, termed a *lead*, nearly in a direct line, appeared for us to escape through. It was fast closing, so that it was evident if we did not instantly proceed and get through this passage, we should certainly be beset. One ship not six miles from us, was observed to be then enclosed in a manner that made its situation very critical at least, and its release extremely uncertain. We fortunately got clear, but soon found other obstacles from an impenetrable barrier extending from the south-east, to the north-west. By observation, we found ourselves in latitude 73° 18' N. longitude 9° W. A month had now been employed in every zealous endeavour to get to the westward, with the hope of there succeeding in the fishery, and in the fullest persuasion that the whales must have taken

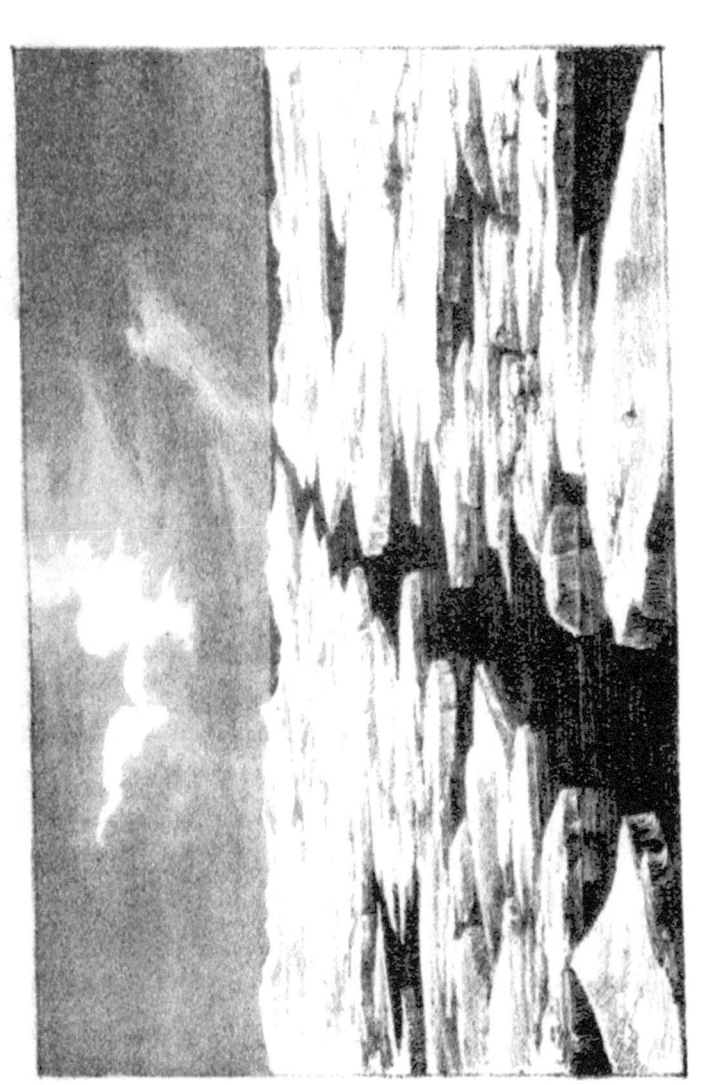

DIRECT LEAD THROUGH PATCH ICE.

that direction. To accomplish this plan, every point of the compass had been tried, every part visited, and every opening pursued until we could proceed no further through the ice. Captain Scoresby on returning from the crow's nest, and the latitude being reported to him, said, "Then, alas! all further attempts to get to the westward are in vain; having only attained fifty miles of western course, very few whales having been seen and none taken, that destination must now be given up, and search made for whales in other situations." I heard the declaration with feelings of the deepest regret, for I had contemplated setting my foot upon that long-lost country of Greenland, which for ages had been shut from all knowledge; and probably upon a part never yet trodden by man; my disappointment was the greater because I had designed to attempt a geographical and hydrographical description of the country, and to collect, as far as my time and limited abilities would permit, other information of importance to science.

We now sailed to the eastward, and the weather being calm, I went in pursuit of a finner, (*Balæna Physalis*, LINN.), with the intention of proving the effect of a shell upon one of those fish, which are allowed to be the most difficult and dangerous to attack, being persuaded that instantaneous destruction would attend the explosion of a shell in the viscera of the animal; but, my expected prey went down, and did not come up within a quarter of a mile from us. This is not only the largest of the whale tribe, but the most powerful of created beings, which from the great danger attending the attack of it, the small produce of blubber, and the inferior quality of the laminæ, roams undisturbed by the fishers. The length of the physalis is stated to be upwards of one hundred feet, and its circumference thirty-five feet. It derives its name from a fin upon its back near the tail; its habits are unlike the mysticetus, for it never rests upon the surface of the water when it comes up to blow, but keeps moving with great speed and activity. Some daring fishers have attempted to take it with a harpoon, but the instant it is struck it sets off with prodigious velocity, soon dragging the boat through the water, beyond the reach of assistance and out of sight of the ship and boats, so that the fishers are obliged to cut the line for their own security. Captain Scoresby stated to me the following particulars of attempts which he had made to capture one of these formidable creatures. " In the year 1818, I ordered a general chase of them, providing against the danger of having my crew separated from the ship, by appointing a rendezvous on the shore not far distant; I prepared also against the loss of much line, by dividing it at two hundred fathoms from the harpoon, and affixing a buoy at the end of it. Thus arranged, one of these whales was shot and another struck: the former dived with such impetuosity, that the line was broken by the resistance of the buoy as soon as it was thrown into the water; and, the latter was liberated in a minute, by the separation of the line, occasioned, it was supposed, by its friction against the dorsal fin. Both of them escaped. Another physalis was struck, but dived with such velocity that four hundred and eighty fathoms of line were drawn from the boat in about a minute of time, and the fish was lost by the breaking of the line."

July 10. Having requested to be called, whenever any thing worthy of observation should occur, I arose at two o'clock A. M., on being informed that a number of seals were seen about two miles from us, on a floe of ice, and at a considerable distance from the water's edge. Being told there was no hole by which they could escape, I calculated on a good booty, and went, like Robinson Crusoe, with my two guns, expecting that the double and single barrels, would secure three; I likewise furnished the boat's crew with seal clubs, but on our approach these sagacious animals retreated one by one through a small hole in the ice to the water, before we got within one hundred and fifty yards of them; and left us to hunt about for the ship for four hours, in very great anxiety, as a dense fog which had arisen instantaneously prevented our seeing beyond twenty yards around us. The fog clearing away about eight o'clock, we continued our course to the eastward until two o'clock, when floes of ice determined that we should proceed no further in that direction; we, therefore, sailed to the northward.

In this course a new scene was presented to us;

a great quantity of bay ice had formed on the edges of the floes, so that being perfectly smooth, and extending like an immense plain, it offered a striking contrast to the ponderous masses of every variety of form and size which rose behind it. The temperature of the atmosphere during the last three days, had been delightful, and the sun now exercised its genial influence on the snow, which covered the fields and floes of ice. In their lowest parts were formed large pools, or lakes, of fresh water, from which tributary offerings were pouring in small channels, through cavities in the edge of the ice, to mingle with the waters of the ocean. A curious effect was produced by the sun's dazzling beams on lofty masses of the ice, whose summits overarched their sides, or had openings in them, from whence long pendent icicles shone with a reflected transparency, the splendour of which nothing could exceed. The mass here exhibited was at least forty feet high and sixty in length.

July 14. The extraordinary fine and warm weather of the ninth and tenth instant, brought its usual consequence in this region; a most dense fog for three successive days, which kept us in much awful anxiety, to discover our situation, as perfect calms and strong breezes had prevailed, both of which are formidable enemies to the navigation of those seas. In the afternoon the fog abated, and we found ourselves in more open water than we had been in for some time. We saw a vessel, appearing to be deeply laden, and to be sailing towards England; we stood towards her to avail ourselves of this opportunity of informing our absent friends, that we were well, had been in ice for more than two months, and had taken very few whales. A boat was despatched with this news; and on its return we found the ship to be the Vigilant of London, which was homeward bound, having had good success, in taking fourteen whales; we also learned that in the boat hanging over its stern was a coffin containing the remains of one of its boat-steerers, who the day before had been killed by a whale while he was performing the dangerous service of lancing it. This, among the many dangers attendant on the Greenland fishing, confirms and clearly shews the advantage that would be derived from the use of shells and carcasses; which, by judicious management and proper application, will at once remove the most dangerous part of the scene by lacerating the vitals, and this in perfect security, at a distance beyond the reach of the most enraged fish. In the evening we saw a shoal of seals sporting upon the surface of the ocean: this the sailors called a *wedding:* and at night we caught a large one, as it was sleeping upon a piece of ice which we were passing.

July 15. The wind having continued a steady breeze all the night, and the ship having kept a northern course, it was calculated (for we had not seen the sun to take an observation,) that we had attained about the 76° of latitude. Here the ice exhibited a wonderful change in its appearance from the powerful influence of the sun, which we had experienced in the commencement of the week; the snow that had generally incrusted its surface, was nearly melted away, and the temperature of the day, the thermometer being at 36, had much contributed to its dissolution. At one o'clock a thick fog set in, but we, being tolerably free from ice, felt less anxiety than is usual on such occasions; about six o'clock the fog cleared, and we changed our course to the westward, determined to try what a higher latitude might produce, but we had not proceeded longer than five hours, when, towards the north-west, the brightest ice blink I had ever seen, stretched across the horizon from the south-west to north-east; I beheld this splendid phenomenon with very great concern, as it foreboded further opposition to the much-desired object of getting to the western land. Being joined by the Experiment of Hull, and the Jean of Peterhead, the masters came on board and gave the sorrowful tidings of the impracticability of getting near the west land, which they had been trying, on the assurance that the whales had resorted to it last year: they stated, that they had endeavoured to effect that object, from the 78° to the 71° of latitude, but that a range of impenetrable ice had compelled them to relinquish the attempt. They also remarked, that the ice had not pursued its usual summer course; that fields and floes were more numerous; that the fields were fixed, and that the floes had not gone to the south. The obstruction to their course appeared to them to have proceeded in a great measure, from a compact body of ice which extended from the island of Jan Mayne to the west-land, and thereby stopping up that outlet, prevented the ice from going by its usual channel to be broken up, or dissolved by the temperature of a milder climate. They made some curious remarks on the difference in the quantity of the ice, observed during this season from that which is generally seen; but particularly in comparison of what they had found in visiting this country last year, when so great a decrease had taken place as to admit ships very near to the west land. This observation was confirmed by Captain Scoresby with the remark, that he was strongly inclined to believe from what he had seen this voyage, that from Point Look-out, to Cape Farewell, the space of ice had augmented by an amount equal to the superficial content of Great Britain.

The masters of the vessels just mentioned were principally induced to come on board for the purpose of requesting to see the means proposed by me for an improvement in the whale fishery; and I was much pleased thus to find that the design of my voyage had publicity among the navigators, now in Greenland. It was no less gratifying to hear the very warm approbation which, on inspecting my implements, they bestowed upon them generally; and more particularly upon my hand harpoon. Of the advantages likely to be derived from this entirely new principle, by which it is impossible for a whale to disengage itself from the weapon, they spoke in the strongest terms possible. The master of the Experiment had already received from the Society of Arts, &c., the premium for having in one season, with a harpoon gun, shot the greatest number of whales. From his great experience therefore in that method of taking whales, I felt no slight degree of satisfaction at the favourable opinion which he gave me of my gun harpoon, of its fully answering the purposes proposed, and of the very great advantage to be derived from its use, now that whales were so difficult to be obtained. It also afforded me great pleasure, to hear both masters express their unqualified confidence that my design to lessen the perils to which whale fishers are often exposed would fully succeed; and that all danger would be removed by the use of the shells and carcasses to destroy the power of the fish. They appeared to be fully impressed with the advantage to be expected from these inventions, from having witnessed, in the pursuit of their avocation, the melancholy fate of some of their companions, who had been suddenly cut off by these powerful monsters of the deep. The death of the boat-steerer, whose corpse was proceeding home in the Vigilant, they particularly described, as the event took place near them; the man was in the act of lancing a whale, when by one powerful swing of its tail, it swept him overboard, and instantly with another tremendous blow deprived him of life, by breaking every rib, and almost every bone in his body. Captain Scoresby also related several extraordinary instances from personal observation, of the destructive power and determined defence of some fish; he spoke of one occasion in particular, in which a whale destroyed every boat as it approached; and he also mentioned the fact, to shew the power of that fish, that, a few years since, a boat belonging to the Ainswell of Whitby was struck by a whale, while the crew were attempting to kill it, and literally shivered to pieces by the blow; of the crew three perished. Numerous similar accidents I have heard described by the commanders of other vessels, on board of which I went during this voyage.

The life of a sailor is at all times precarious, and deserving the serious regard of every man who is a well-wisher to his country; for sailors, by their honourable and useful exertions, have been the essential means of raising Britain above the rest of the world, in commerce and in naval power. But, there is a particular solicitude due to those who gain their subsistence from the Greenland fishery, as they are exposed to dangers which have often proved fatal, from masses of floating ice crushing the vessels to pieces, or sinking them beneath their frightful weight; while they also encounter great hazards in their employment, of capturing the monsters of the deep for the use of man. There is, perhaps, no class of men more eminently useful than they who prosecute this branch of commerce; and, certainly, none whose employment is attended with so many difficulties, dangers, and privations. Their toils are extremely fatiguing, and their avocation subjects them to a variety of unavoidable hardships; they are totally excluded from the comforts known to most other seamen; and, above all, they endure the extreme severity of rigorous cold. Should the severe calamity of sickness or accident occur while on this voyage, their situation becomes extremely pitiable, as the accommodation of a Greenland ship is little calculated to alleviate sufferings; nor is the supply of vegetable food such as sickness might require. Those who possess a spark of philanthropy must therefore feel for the situation of these men, and will not withhold from them their keenest sympathy.

July 10. On this Sunday a large bear was observed upon a piece of ice which we passed: Bruin looked at us, and took no other notice, but marched on, snuffing the breeze, as if conscious of the protection which the day afforded him, or, confident of his own power if attacked.

July 16. The fog that had prevailed during the night, cleared away in the morning, and the fleet as well as ourselves, sailed from latitude 76° to the westward, and continued going in that direction fourteen hours, when we came to a barrier of ice that extended from south to north in a westerly direction, and of an extent beyond our power to ascertain. It is impossible for language to describe the disappointment which we suffered at having our progress again arrested, and the effect which the solitary and dreary aspect of this icy continent produced upon our minds, from its situation beyond the limits of the habitable globe, from the profound silence that prevailed upon this domain of desolation, and, more particularly, from its opposing defiance to our proceeding.

While we were indulging in these gloomy reflections, an immense bear, (*Ursus Albus,*) made its appearance at about half a mile distant from us, from behind one of the large hummocks that were resting upon the margin of the ice.

I instantly seized my gun, jumped into a boat with its crew, was lowered down, and went after it; but in vain, as it took the hint, and moved off across the ice, which was so thickly covered with the most rugged hummocks that it was impossible to overtake it. I could not help feeling astonished at the rapidity with which this animal travelled, as well as the extraordinary size of the tracks which it left in the snow, and which from curiosity I measured, and found the length of the impression of the hind paw to be one foot ten inches, and its breadth one foot, and that of the fore paw one foot one inch in length, and one foot in breadth. A fog hastily came on, which, though it hid the bear from our sight, gave us the opportunity long after, of hearing his loud growlings; whether they proceeded from disappointment at not having attained the food of which he was in search, or whether they were love strains to apprize some favourite of his approach, I must leave to more competent judges to determine.

July 17. The fog dispersing at eight o'clock in the morning, we endeavoured to proceed round a compact *patch** of ice that impeded us in our western course; several unicorns were seen, and I went in a boat after them without success, as they retired under the ice. I waited their return for some time, but they were too shy to allow a harpoon to be thrown into them; I therefore fired a shell at one that was rapidly passing along at some distance, having an extraordinary large horn; but it passed about an inch above his back, and after repeatedly bounding from the surface of the water, it burst at least half a mile distant.

Just as we were sitting down to dinner, the man at the mast head, called out that a great bear had

---

* A compact patch of ice, is a collection of pieces of considerable magnitude with openings among them, the extent of which patch is visible.

COMPACT PATCH ICE.

London, Pub. by G. & W.B. Whittaker, Ave Maria Lane.

just quitted the ice and was in the sea. On hearing this, I instantly requested a boat, and went after him. Seeing that he was going leisurely to a large floe of ice at some distance, we got within a hundred yards of him before we were noticed; when he instantly turned to endeavour to regain the ice, and we rowed with all our might to cut him off: finding that he failed in his object, he changed his route to face the boat, and approached it, keeping up a continued growling with other indications of rage, such as shewing his frightful teeth, and elevating his head and much of his body out of the water. Being desirous to preserve the head of an animal represented to be of an unusual size, I let him come within twelve yards, when I fired a ball through his shoulder, which deprived him of the use of a fore leg, when he roared hideously, pressed towards us in the most ferocious manner, and endeavoured to board or upset the boat, but failed from the loss of his leg: he was then attacked by the crew with lances, the thrusts of some of which he avoided with astonishing dexterity, and, in the most resolute manner, again made several attempts to reach the boat, but being repulsed by an overpowering thrust of a lance from the harpooner on his flank, he was unable longer to hold the contest. During its continuance he had bitten a lance with such exasperated rage, as to break one of his long tusks: finding battle fruitless in the water, he retreated towards the ice, swimming most astonishingly fast, considering the great propelling power which he had lost from the wound in his fore leg; he reached the ice, which he ascended with great difficulty, having only one fore paw to assist him. Determined to injure the skin as little as possible, and to attack him in front, I got upon the ice, and was about to fire another ball to free him from his sufferings, when he uttered a tremendous growl, and fell down dead: as it now began to snow very fast, no time was lost in launching, towing, and hoisting him on board the ship; he proved of a size much larger than usually seen, and the following are the particulars of his measurement:

	Feet	Inches
Length from the snout to the tail .	7	6
Height of the shoulder	4	6
Circumference at the shoulder . .	6	$11\frac{1}{2}$
Breadth of the fore paw	0	$11\frac{1}{2}$
Breadth of the hind paw	0	$9\frac{1}{2}$
Length of the fore claws	0	$2\frac{3}{4}$
Length of the hind claws	0	$2\frac{1}{4}$
Length of the tusks in the upper jaw	0	$2\frac{1}{8}$

The general character of the great polar bear, is a long narrow head and neck; tip of the nose black; teeth of hideous magnitude; hair of a great length, soft and white, and in some parts tinged with yellow; limbs very thick and strong; ears short and rounded; front teeth six, both above and below; two lateral teeth of the lower jaw longer than the rest, and lobed with small or secondary teeth at the internal base; canine teeth solitary; grinders on each side, the first approximated to the canine teeth; tongue smooth; snout prominent; eyes small and furnished with a military membrane. Mr. Pennant, speaking of the polar bear says, "those which are brought alive to England, are always in motion, restless, and furious, but in a state of nature they are dreadfully ferocious. They will attack and attempt to board armed vessels, far distant from the shore, and have been with great difficulty repelled. They seem to give a preference to human blood, and will greedily tear up the graves of the buried to devour the cadaverous contents." I have collected the following interesting historical particulars, concerning this ferocious animal. The polar bear is considered the natural lord of these regions: he preys indiscriminately on quadrupeds, fowls, reptiles, and fishes; these all behold him with dread and flee his presence, as his approach is the signal of immediate destruction. The seals either retire to their submarine dwellings, or conceal themselves in the crevices of the ice; while he, stalking along with solemn majesty, faces the breeze, raises his head, and snuffs the passing scent, until he discovers the nearest route to his odorous banquet. Thomson thus beautifully describes him:

———————— The shapeless bear,
With dangling ice all horrid, stalks forlorn;
Slow-paced, and sourer, as the storms increase.
He makes his bed beneath the inclement drift,
And, with stern patience, scorning weak complaint,
Hardens his heart against assailing want.

The bear is possessed of uncommon strength, and when beset, defends itself with most extraordinary obstinacy. A particular instance is thus related by Captain Lewis: "A party of six hunters attacked a bear, and when at the distance of forty yards, four of them fired, and each lodged a musket-ball in its body, two of which passed directly through the lungs. The justly enraged animal ran at them with open mouth, and as it came near, the two men who had reserved their fire gave it two wounds, and broke its shoulder, which retarded its motion for a moment, but before they could re-load, it was so near, that they were obliged to run to the river, and before they reached it, the bear had almost overtaken them: two jumped into the canoe, the other four separated, concealed themselves and fired as fast as they could load; they struck it several times, but this only exasperated it; and at last, it pursued two of them so closely, that they jumped down a perpendicular bank of twenty feet in height into the water; the bear sprang after them, and was within a few feet of the hindermost, when one of the hunters on shore, shot it in the head and killed it. They dragged it to the shore, and found that eight balls had passed through its body." In many instances, the bear has been said to have attacked persons, when not opposed, and an interesting narrative of that fact is related by Barentz in his voyage in search of a north-east passage to China. In the island of Nova Zembla, the bears attacked his men, seizing them in their mouths, carrying them off, and devouring them in the sight of their companions. "On the sixth of September," observes this interesting writer, "some sailors landed to seek for a certain sort of stone; during the search, two of them were sleeping, one by the other, when a white bear approached them softly, and seized one of them by the back of his neck; the sailor not knowing what it was, cried out, 'Who has seized me there behind?' when the other raised his head, exclaimed, 'Halloo! it is a bear!' and immediately rose up, and ran away. The bear bit the unfortunate man in several parts of the head, and after having quite mangled him sucked his blood. The rest of the persons who were on shore, to the number of twenty, immediately ran with fire locks and pikes, and found the bear devouring the body. On seeing the men, he ran towards them with incredible fury, threw himself upon one of them, carried him away, and tore him to pieces, which so terrified them that the rest all fled. Those who remained in the vessel seeing them thus flee, and return towards the shore, jumped into a boat, and rowed with all their force to receive them; when they had landed and beheld the lamentable spectacle, they encouraged the others to return with them to the combat, that all together they might attack the ferocious animal. Three of them advanced a little; the bear still continuing to devour his prey, without being at all disturbed at the sight of thirty men so near him. The two pilots having fired three times without hitting the animal, the purser shot him in the head close by the eye, which did not cause him to quit his prey; but he continued holding the body by the neck, and devouring it. After several other attacks being made, he was killed. The two half-devoured bodies were interred in the Isle of Slates, and the skin of the bear was carried to Amsterdam."

Other instances, which have occurred not many years since, exemplify the strength and ferocity of the polar bear: a whale ship was moored to a piece of ice in Davis's Straits, and the crew were all in the ship with the exception of one man who had strayed some distance on the ice; a bear approached him unobserved, seized him by the thigh, and carried him away before he could be rescued. It is also related, that as a ship was lying by the side of the ice, a bear came on board, and compelled the crew who were on the deck, to get upon the rigging to preserve themselves. Instances have also occurred, in which bears have not only upset the boats from which they were attacked, but have even got on board of them and compelled the crews to jump overboard, and leave them in possession. In the year 1783, Captain Cook of the Archangel, of Lynn, being on the coast of Spitzbergen, landed, accompanied by his surgeon and mate; while traversing the shore, the Captain was unexpectedly attacked by a bear, which seized him in an instant between its paws: at this awful juncture when a moment's pause must have been fatal to him, he called to his surgeon to fire; who, with admirable resolution and steadiness, discharged his piece, and providentially shot the bear through the head. The Captain by this prompt assistance was preserved from being torn in pieces. Three years since Captain Hawkins, of the Everthope of Hull, nearly lost his life in attacking a bear. The animal defended himself with wonderful fury, and succeeded in getting into the boat; then seized Mr. Hawkins by the thigh, dragged him overboard, and swam away with him to some distance, before he let him go: the animal no doubt would have destroyed him, had he not been pursued by the boat.

Many similar instances were related to me, during my voyage, by persons who had witnessed the astonishing strength and ferocity of the polar bear: it may almost be classed among amphibious animals, not only as being an excellent swimmer but an expert diver. During the summer months, allured by the scent of the carcasses of whales, seals, &c., these bears make excursions on the ice, on which they have been found more than eighty miles from land: they have also been seen going through the sea, from one piece of ice to another six miles distant. During the winter they return to land, and bury themselves deep beneath the snow, or in caverns formed in the ice; here, they pass the long and dreary arctic winter, and do not again appear until the return of spring.

July 19. The wind being west, we spent the whole day in beating to windward, but without making the land, though we often imagined that we saw it. The appearances which thus deceived us, proved to be nothing more than *cape-fly-aways*, as the sailors term them, or clouds resembling distant land. After a few hours' sailing, the water assumed the colour known to afford the favourite food to whales, for which, therefore, every one now anxiously looked. It was singular that we had now voyaged some thousands of miles, with the colour of the water as blue as indigo, which may in some measure account for the small number of whales that we had seen: and those few, were not resident but running fish, that is, travelling from one place to another. The temperature of this day was most delightful; the thermometer was at 40°, latitude by observation, 74° 64', N., longitude 12° W.

July 21. After a strong gale from the westward during the whole of yesterday, accompanied by thick weather, which prevented our making much progress, the wind this morning abated, and changed to the south-east; by noon the weather became clear, and enabled us not only to pursue our course but to observe our situation; we were at the entrance of a very deep bay formed by the most extensive fields of ice, with which we had hitherto met; they extended very far beyond the reach of natural vision or command of the telescope from the mast-head, and in them neither crack nor fissure could be seen. They were unusually rugged, and encumbered with larger masses of solid ice than I had before seen, and

LARUS PARASITICUS OR ARCTIC GULL.
London. Publ.d by G.& W.B. Whittaker, Ave Maria Lane.

which set limits to human exertion, and defied perseverance to penetrate any distance. Here my mind was satisfied on the formation of this body of ice, it being apparent that those immense rugged spaces which we observed, had received their inequality of surface by the hard pressure of immense pieces coming in contact, and uniting by the strong congealing power, during the long arctic winter, in which there is no sun to abate its rigour.

This ice is said to be similar in nature and character to that which extends to the North Pole, and which hitherto has prevented any successful expedition to that interesting part of the world. Having requested a boat for an exploring and a shooting expedition, I observed near the verge of the ice, the track of some animal, and on examination, found it resembled that of a small dog; the impression was quite round, and the footsteps followed each other in a direct line; it probably was an arctic fox, *Canis Lagopus*, (LINN.) In the course of the day, several kittywakes at a great distance were heard to make an uncommon screaming, which, on coming nearer to them, I found to proceed from the appearance of some *Larus Parasiticus*, (LINN.,) or arctic Gulls: these gulls feed on fish that have been caught by other birds, whom they persecute until they oblige them to drop their prey, and then with astonishing dexterity they catch it before it reaches the water: these birds live by plunder, and display a great deal of cunning in watching the flight of ducks, and other aquatic birds from their nests, when they instantly occupy them and devour their eggs. After several ineffectual attempts to procure one of these marauders, I at length succeeded in shooting one which came within reach of my gun. This bird is called by Buffon, *l'abbé-à-longue-queue*; it is singularly beautiful and elegant; it has a black bill one inch and a quarter in length from the base; upper mandible most curved at the point; lower mandible gibbous; nostril, linear and situated in a curve; tongue cleft; front, crown, and nape dark brown; neck, cheeks, chin, throat, breast and belly, white; all the rest of the body dusky; wings, darker coloured; the two middle feathers of the tail, seven inches longer than the rest; legs, lead-colour; thighs, black; and feet of the same hue and webbed; length nineteen inches; extent of wing, thirty-nine inches; insides, amber brown.

On returning on board, an unicorn was observed upon the surface of the water, in a very unusual posture, exhibiting one of the lobes of its tail, while a fin occasionally moved; on getting nearer to it, it was distinctly seen to be lying on its side, and supporting by its fin a little one, which was sucking at the breast; both the parent and her offspring made their escape just before the harpooner could execute his design of causing a fatal separation between them. The colour of the water continued to deepen, as we proceeded to the westward, and an uncommon quantity of different medusæ was observed floating in it. Medusæ are considered to be both the principal, and the favourite, food of the whale; and, according to Captain Scoresby, it was these animalculæ which here gave colour to the ocean. That which appeared to me the most curious among their varieties, was the medusa pileus; it consisted of eight lobes, with a beautiful iridescent finny fringe on the external edge of each; and in the canal that penetrated them I observed a reddish fluid which moved through it, in the manner that blood is shewn to circulate in a pulse glass. The very favourable appearance of the water excited great surprise that no whales had been seen in it, but the most experienced persons among us supposed, that the fish had been living luxuriously, (traces of them being visible on the surface of the water,) and had proceeded to the westward. This increased our anxiety to pursue that course, and almost determined us to persevere in despite of the lateness of the season, and other local impediments, such as dense fogs, which are attendant on this period of the year. The ships that had been our companions for some time, now began to evince a hopelessness in the minds of their commanders, for about mid-day, we saw them change their course, and steer to the eastward. Knowing by a previous observation taken by Captain Scoresby, that we could not now be more than twenty or thirty miles from the land, which the fog consequently alone hid from our sight, we went to the bottom of the bay, determined to leave no effort untried where there was the slightest probability of success; but we found that the ice formed a complete and impenetrable barrier, with its boundary on each side presenting impediments wholly unconquerable. The ice forming this bay, from some cause, known only to Him who gives laws to the universe, indicated a general movement; and we lost no time in beating out; when this was accomplished, we sailed to the southward. In this proceeding a very rapid movement of the ice became evident, obstacles kept increasing that caused us much alarm, and prevented us from keeping our course; from prudence, as well as necessity, we were obliged to pay deference to these immense bodies of ice, by making room for them to pass, particularly, as a dense fog was coming on that soon prevented our seeing fifty yards from the ship. The fog continuing, the ship was moored to a floe piece of ice, on which was a fine pool of water, from whence several casks were filled for the ship's use: this water was of the finest quality possible, having been produced by the melted snow and ice, and from its not containing animalculæ, it had the property of keeping for any length of time.

July 22. Still wrapped in the thickest mist: just after evening prayers it was discovered that floes of ice were surrounding us in a manner which excited considerable alarm; every exertion was made to free ourselves, and happily, we found a space of water where the ship could for a time float in safety.

July 23. The weather was perfectly calm, with an extremely dense fog; and the sounds of crashing ice gave threatenings of the liability of our being beset; at length a heavy piece, the extent of which could not be discovered, was seen not two ships' length from us, and consequently the most powerful exertion of the crew in towing, with all the other efforts used on such occasions, was employed to keep clear of it. The effect produced by immense masses coming in contact with each other resembled heavy cannonading at a distance; the sound was at once awful, and sublimely grand. At noon the weather began to clear, though not sufficiently to take an observation from the deck; but Captain Scoresby, whose resources seemed inexhaustible, attained his object by measuring from the mast head the altitude of the sun from its reflected image upon the water, which was so smooth as to act the part of a mirror: our latitude, thus ascertained, was found to be 74° 30′ N. and longitude 12° W. This made me still more anxious for clear weather, as from our situation we ought to see the west land. At six o'clock in the evening the fog began to disperse, and in two hours I had the gratification of seeing, about forty-five miles distant, the land on the eastern side of old or lost Greenland.

This remote region called by geographers of northern countries, West Greenland, is presumed to reach from the southernmost point of Cape Farewell and Statenbrook on the right side, in the 60th degree of north latitude, north-east towards Spitzbergen as far as the 80th degree of north latitude. This eastern side is almost totally un-

L

known, being rendered inaccessible by the great quantity of floating ice which, probably forming a compact body to the land, prevents all communication with it: the distance was too far and the weather not sufficiently clear to enable me to ascertain the precise nature of the coast; but by the aid of a good glass and much attention, I succeeded in making a correct resemblance of its character, so as to distinguish its features, determine the great evenness of the surface of its mountains, the singular point of one, and the ruggedness of another: I could also plainly see that the snow was confined

only to its valleys, that there was none upon its loftier lands, and that the face of these last did not wear the appearance of sterile rock, but was veined with variegated colours, as if spread over with a little earth, turf, or a scanty covering of vegetation. A prospect like this greatly interested me, being persuaded that many valuable objects of natural history would consequently be furnished by these regions. The range of country which I could distinguish extended from north-west, to north-north-west, and uniformly bore the same character.

The only history of this almost unknown land, and particularly of the eastern side, is, that it was first peopled by Icelanders in the tenth century, but their colonization did not extend to the southern limits of the arctic circle; they soon became a thriving colony, and bestowed on their new habitation the name of Groenland, or Greenland. This colony was converted to Christianity by a missionary from Norway, sent thither by the celebrated Olaf, the first Norwegian monarch who embraced the Christian religion. The Greenland settlement continued to increase and thrive under his protection; and, in a little time, the country was provided with many towns, churches, convents, bishops, &c., under the jurisdiction of the archbishop of Drontheim. A considerable commerce was carried on between Greenland and Norway; and a regular intercourse maintained between the two countries till the year 1406, when the last bishop was sent over. About this time, by the gradual increase of the arctic ice, the colony appears to have been completely imprisoned in the frozen ocean; while on the west a range of impassable mountains and plains, covered with perpetual ice and snow, precluded all access. The ancient settlement may be traced in the map of Torfaeus in his *Groenlandia Antiqua;* from which it would seem that the colony extended over about two hundred miles in the southeast extremity of Greenland. On the west, some ruins of churches have also been discovered. About a hundred years after all intercourse between Norway and Greenland had ceased, several ships were sent successively by the kings of Denmark, in order to discover the eastern district, but all of them miscarried. Among these adventurers, Magus Hennisen, after having surmounted many difficulties and dangers, got sight of the land, which, however, he could not approach. At his return, he pretended that the ship had been arrested in the middle of her course by rocks of load-stone at the bottom of the sea.

The same year, 1576, in which this attempt was made, Captain Martin Frobisher was sent on the same errand by Queen Elizabeth. He likewise descried the land; but finding it so difficult of approach, returned to England; but not before he had sailed sixty leagues in the strait which retains his name, and landed on several islands, where he had some communications with the natives. He had likewise taken possession of the country in the name of Queen Elizabeth; and brought away some pieces of ore, from which the refiners of London extracted a proportion of gold. In the ensuing spring, he undertook a second voyage at the head of a small squadron equipped at the expense of the public; entered the straits again; discovered upon an island a gold and silver mine; bestowed names upon different bays, islands, and headlands; and brought away a lading of ore, together with two natives, a male and a female. Such was the success of this voyage, that another squadron was fitted out under the command of the same officer, with the rank of admiral; it consisted of fifteen ships, including a considerable number of soldiers, miners, smelters, carpenters, &c., who were to remain all the winter in a wooden fort, the different pieces of which they carried out in the transports. They met with boisterous weather, impenetrable fogs, and violent currents, which retarded their operations until the season was too far advanced. The Admiral therefore determined to return with as much ore as he could procure: of this they obtained large quantities out of a new mine, to which they gave the name of the Countess of Sussex. They set sail in the beginning of September, and after a month's stormy passage, arrived in England; but this adventure was never after prosecuted.

Thus stood the affairs of Greenland, when Hans Egede, minister of Vogen in Norway, prompted by a laudable zeal to promote the knowledge of Christ among the savage Greenlanders, made some proposals for renewing the intercourse between Denmark and Norway, and Greenland, which had been discontinued for many centuries. Most of the friends and acquaintances of this worthy divine, when they heard of his project, looked upon it as a chimerical undertaking. However, in 1718, he resigned his benefice in the south part of Norway, and removed with his wife and children to Bergen. His proposals did not meet with a favourable reception, either from the merchants or clergy of that city; he therefore went to Copenhagen in 1719, and laid his plan before the king; who sent an order to the magistrates of Bergen, to propose to the citizens the erecting of a Greenland company. This, after many difficulties, was at last effected in 1721, and a capital of ten thousand rix-dollars was raised for that purpose.

The new established company fitted out three ships for Greenland, and the indefatigable Egede was sent thither as missionary, furnished with three hundred guilders by the society for propagating the gospel at Copenhagen. It was not without great danger and difficulty, that the single ship which had the missionary on board, at length arrived off Baal's river, on the west side of Greenland, and wintered in an island there. M. Egede and forty men that remained with him, immediately set about building a house, in which the natives readily assisted them. The new colony, thus commenced, was from year to year carefully supplied with necessaries by the company; but the trade carried on with Greenland brought in no great profit. In the mean time, the missionary employed his time in learning the Greenland language, and by his liberality and suavity of manners so endeared himself to the inhabitants, that the respect they showed him in some particulars far exceeded his wishes, for they entertained such an exalted idea of his piety and virtue, that all the sick flocked about him imploring him to heal them, being persuaded that his breathing on them would restore them to health. His Danish majesty, in 1728, caused horses to be transported to New Greenland, in hopes that the settlers might thereby travel over land to Eastern or Old Greenland. Lieutenant Richards, in a ship which had wintered near the new Danish colony, also attempted on his return to Denmark, to land in Old Greenland, but all his efforts proved abortive. M. Egede gave it as his opinion that the only practicable method of reaching that part of the country, would be to coast north about in small vessels, between the great ice fields and the shore ; as the Greenlanders had declared that the currents which rush continually from the bays and inlets, and run southwestward along the shore, prevent the ice from adhering to the land, so that there is always a channel open, through which vessels of small burden might pass, especially if lodges were built at proper distances on the shore, for the convenience and direction of the adventurers. In 1731, a royal edict was published enjoining all the king's subjects in Greenland to return home; and the colonies were thereby dissolved. But M. Egede, being zealous for the salvation of the inhabitants, staid behind, together with his family and some others who chose to follow his fortunes. This zealous man who was called the arctic apostle, feeling a deep desire to explore the eastern side, accompanied some Greenlanders, who went fifty leagues for the purpose of catching deer, to determine if it was practicable; and, on the 2d of September, 1751, he fitted out an expedition from the west side to explore the opposite boundary; when, having passed over much uneven ice, full of clefts, he was compelled to relinquish the enterprise after five days' toil, the particulars of which are thus related: " About north-east, or east north-east, are the nearest hills on the eastern side; they are less than those on the west side, which I supposed from hence, because they were covered with snow. The country where Frobisher's strait is imagined to be, appeared pretty much above the level, and constantly covered with ice. I do not know that I saw more than two or three little hills that could be supposed land; on the contrary, towards the north-east, and north-west, the rocks plainly rear their heads above the ice, and some of the tops are entirely naked of snow; I saw particularly one long hill between two huge rocks, whose bare backs looked altogether of the natural colour of the earth. Were I to give my sentiments of this whole icy region, that cuts off the communication with the east side, I should imagine that as far as relates to the way, the journey might be practicable; for the plains of ice did not seem so dangerous, or the pits in it so deep as they are said to be."

The whale fishery having, until a few years since, been confined to the northward, about the latitude of 78° north, and never exceeding the longitude of 2° west, no ships consequently ever approached near the coast of Greenland. Captain Scoresby, however, deviating from the accustomed track of the whale fishers, in 1817, penetrated into the western ice, and made the same land seen by us this day, and which appears to be that discerned, in 1654, by Gaal Hamkes, and which is laid down in modern charts and called after its discoverer. The position of the ice having lately been observed to have much opened to the west, the whale fishers extended their pursuit to that point of the compass; and during the fishing season of last year, the ice had sufficiently moved away, to admit not only of the land being seen, but to leave no impediment to the approach towards it. Captain Scoresby, indeed, was so near the shore, that he had an opportunity of landing; but the concerns of the fishing which necessarily occupied his first attention, prevented him from making those investigations and surveys which he would have gladly undertaken. This year he had hoped that the fishing might have led him again to the coast, and that some lucky circumstance might have afforded him an opportunity (without trespassing on the duties of his voyage) of ascertaining the fate of the lost colony, and of fixing the position of the most remarkable points of land. I had also an earnest intention to have gathered such correct geographical descriptions as were in my power, and to have made a faithful delineation of every circumstance interesting to the philosopher and naturalist.

I cannot take my leave of this part of the unknown world, without expressing my anxious desire to exalt the fame of my country in discovery. And although disappointed of being among those who are to take possession of lost Greenland;—to delineate the extent of the country, which, from measurement by latitude and longitude is more than five hundred thousand square miles; to ascertain whether it forms a part of the continent of America in a continued line, or whether it is an island or an archipelago of islands; and lastly, whether considerable national advantage would not be derived from its productions, in promoting the interests of commerce; —I yet consider it my bounden duty to submit it, as worthy the attention of those who direct the affairs of state, to promote such an undertaking, in prosecuting which great national benefit might also be derived in the improvement of the whale fishery. An expedition of two ships, I have ascertained, might be sent out fully equipped for 8,000*l*. or 10,000*l*., capable of performing a voyage of six or eight months; but if it were permitted that the fishing might be conducted in such intervals as could not be appropriated to discovery, the expense would possibly be reduced to 6,000*l*. In the success of such an expedition, I am most sanguine, and, were I blessed with fortune, I would not wish to increase the burdens of my country with the expense, but gladly bear the charge of the undertaking, in the confident expectation that much valuable information would be derived, beneficial to mankind, and honourable to the fame of England.

July 24. A brighter sun never illumined the earth, than was attendant on the icy regions all this day, and Captain Scoresby observing the appearance of the moon, devoted his time to taking lunar observations to correct his chronometer, to discover the longitude of this unknown land, and to make other experiments and scientific observations. Among them, I must not omit the use of an instrument called a *magnitimeter*, invented by him for measuring magnetic attraction, and finding the dip of the needle: some extremely curious experiments were likewise made on the magnetic laws relative to the production, and annihilation of magnetism in iron, by percussion; and on a recent discovery of the precise effect on iron bars, becoming magnetical by position. It is certainly one of the most ingenious instruments I ever saw, and its utility was clearly proved to me in repeated experiments, which, in the science of navigation, must be pre-eminently important. The combined attraction of the iron in the ship, influencing the compass placed near it, was determined also in the most satisfactory manner by comparing the polarity of the compass in the crow's nest, with that in the binnacle, or place where the compass is kept on the ship's deck.

There being but very little wind, I went in pursuit of unicorns, and to shoot aquatic birds; and I succeeded in procuring some good specimens. On my return to the ship, my attention was called by Captain Scoresby to an extraordinary instance of refraction; it was visible to the naked eye, but with a telescope the effect produced by it was astonishing: the atmosphere was particularly clear, the sun extremely bright, and a gentle breeze blowing from the south-west, when, on looking over the western horizon, there appeared to ascend from the distant surface of the ocean, a perpendicular cliff, as if formed of the most regular basaltes of several feet in height. This phenomenon, so very extraordinary and singularly beautiful in these regions, is produced by two streams of air of different temperatures, which occasion an irregular deposition of imperfectly condensed vapour, passing the verge of the horizon.

July 25. Had not the ship been surrounded by ice, it would not have been possible to conceive that we were in the arctic regions, for a brighter sun never shone in England, and the thermometer, influenced by its beams, was at 66°. Its genial warmth animated the creatures of this frozen sea, and the ides of July brought with them their attendant consequences. The powerful blowings of unicorns were heard on every side, the males were chasing the females, and all were in an unusual state of gaiety. Such was the astonishing transparency of the sea, that I distinctly observed a narwal, at least a hundred feet below the surface, and not only saw it turn upon its side to look at the boat, but could afterwards plainly discover that it was a female fish. After coming to the surface several times in the most sportive manner, it at length rose upwards of thirty yards from the boat, when I fired a harpoon from my small gun designed only for shells; but the excessive impetus of the discharge broke the shackle, and knocked me over the boat's thwart, without any injury, however, beyond a slight bruise. From this accident, I had the misfortune to lose the fish, for the gun having entangled the rope, the sharp part of the shackle cut it, but the harpoon and part of the line went about ten yards through the fish, it bled profusely, and the quantity of oily substance that exuded from the wound, brought many mulemacks to regale upon its overflowings; just before the fish died it rose, and lay quietly until we approached near it; but from the clumsiness of the man who had the harpoon ready to strike it, he missed his object, and it sank to rise no more. I, however, staid some time in the hope of its re-appearance, and despatched the boat that came to my assistance in pursuit of two other narwals that I had seen lying upon the surface, about a quarter of a mile distant; and one of which the crew succeeded in capturing. In the dissection of this fish, I had an opportunity of collecting from the stomach, specimens of its favourite food, which I found to be shrimps, and the sepia, or ink fish, of the latter of which I was enabled to procure some excellent specimens before described. On opening the head, I found a concealed tooth embedded in the right side; it presented a rough surface, was solid throughout, and at the extremity had an irregular knob resembling that of a pocket pistol. Seeing a great number of narwals playing about, I went after them without success, but shot many birds on my return to the ship, which was not until past one o'clock in the morning, when the sun was exercising its greatest influence, and actually burning one side of my face, while the opposite was quite chilled;

at this time I observed the ice to generate very fast upon the surface of the water.

Soon after my return, I regretted to hear that Captain Scoresby had been grossly insulted by one of the men, on his reproving him for leaving his watch and being below. This I found to be a serious evil, to which the commanders of vessels in the merchant service are not only liable, but to which they repeatedly subject themselves, for the want of regulations to ensure good order, there being now no remedy beyond setting the offender to some duty. It is an injury of the highest importance to those concerned in the maritime commerce of the country ; and that class of persons, who contribute so importantly to the public exigencies, would derive essential benefit if some laws were provided sufficient to ensure a proper state of discipline and subordination.

July 28. A thick fog having set in, on the evening of the 25th, and continued until this morning with a calm, and the ice being in great motion, we were kept in a continued state of anxiety and very great alarm for the safety of the ship, as it was impossible to see twice its length around us, and boats were constantly employed to guard us against the continued impediments which were coming in our way, such as fixed fields, floating floes, islands of ice, as well as immense masses which were lying in the most troublesome manner possible to intercept our course. At length, in the morning watch the fog dispersed, we discerned a lead, and there being a strong breeze we availed ourselves of its advantage; in a difficult part of the navigation, the main-top gallant yard was carried away by a brace running foul. Our course was now south-east, and about mid-day we fell in with the Exmouth, which changed its course to be again our companion. In the navigation of this most dangerous sea, it is from the perilous qualities of the ice, a matter of great consolation to have a vessel in company, because in the event of one ship being crushed by the pressure of the ice, it must be abandoned by the crew, who, if another helping hand were not nigh, nor any retreat attainable, would perish from the rigour of the climate.

The wind increasing, and the weather getting clear, we had a fine and rapid run to the eastward, through the mazy windings of the ice, making upwards of seven degrees of longitude in the space of the day. Just before the mid-watch was set a ship was seen sailing towards us, which, on hailing, we found to be the Eber of Hull, one of the vessels which we had, on the 14th of June, seen beset in the ice; we also heard that our fears respecting the ships which we then observed to be in a precarious state were not groundless, as the sides of this vessel had been much crushed in, while held for several days in frozen durance in so perilous a situation, that all its boats were hove out upon the ice, in preparation for the fatal consequences which were expected.

July 30. The fog having continued without abatement yesterday, now gradually changed from the densest mist into the clearest sky. The whole of this day, we continued to sail to windward, with a fresh breeze from the south-east, to keep clear of the heavy bodies of ice, that had so long interrupted us; until, at length, at four o'clock in the afternoon, we could proceed no further for these frozen impediments: we were therefore obliged to retrace our steps, as the only means of seeking some new lead to clear us from the entanglement of those compact bodies of ice that were surrounding us. In the evening I saw two arctic gulls pursue a kittywake, in as systematic a mode of attack as I ever beheld in the flight of the best trained hawks after a heron.

August 1. The fog, returning during the night, added to the very cross pieces and heavy floes of ice that were continually coming in our way, increased the impediments which opposed our getting near the verge of the ice, or boundary called the sea stream, as we were desirous to do in the prosecution of our design of gaining a situation more favourable for fishing. It may be interesting here to give some idea of the obstructions, and the great increase of ice with which we had to contend above what is usually found. The Baffin last year left the west ice, came through that expansive body stretching from east to west in forty-eight hours, and met with very little interruption. We had now been fourteen days making every effort, availing ourselves of every advantage, yet meeting with continual difficulties, opposed to perpetual obstacles, almost in hourly expectation of being beset by the ice, and still within the grasp and dread of floes. In a direct line we had forced our way for 200 miles through these massive floating bodies, and yet were not clear of them, a circumstance not only rare, but never before heard of; and, what is still more unusual, we had passed through the favourite haunts of whales, and often with the advantage of the best water, and yet not one had been seen. The further we approached towards the south in making our easting, the more plainly did the ice exhibit the powerful effect of the sun's irresistible beams, by its being greatly reduced in quantity, and by the snow upon its surface lying in a state of dissolution. I also observed several huge pieces separate by the summer warmth, and tumble headlong into the deep. While we were on a shooting expedition, it rained for the first time since we entered the arctic circle.

In the course of our progress this day, I observed a *Larus Crepidatus*, (black-toed gull, or Dung Bird,) stoop at a large flock of kittywakes, which were seated on the water. The habits of this bird, are similar to those of the *Larus Parasiticus*, by its attacking the kittywakes, evidently to induce them to get on wing, no doubt, in order to pursue them, until they give up the food which they had been collecting: from this system of plunder the *Larus Crepidatus*, as well as the *Parasiticus*, has acquired the name of Dung Bird, from an erroneous notion, that both pursue the kittywakes, to obtain the excrement of the fugitive: but I observed them to harass the latter, until from fatigue, or fear, the kittywake was compelled to disgorge the contents of its stomach, which the pursuer caught with astonishing dexterity before they reached the water, and then the kittywake was no longer molested. The *Larus Crepidatus* has much white about its head and neck, breast and belly; its two central tail feathers are a little longer than the rest, and are black, tipped with white, as are the tips of the wings.

August 4. A perplexing fog with floes of ice having surrounded us, during the last two days we could make very little progress, and were kept in perpetual anxiety and watchful apprehension for the ship's safety; and during the long haziness we lost our companion. This day at noon, the fog began to disperse, and the floes, we were enabled to observe, had not only diminished in number but in size. The ice, indeed, altogether now wore a very different appearance from that which it had hitherto presented: it had lost its beautiful snowy whiteness, as well as the character and forms which it had formerly assumed, with an ever-changing variety, that afforded unceasing gratification, and tended to render a voyage to Greenland much more interesting than to any other part of the world. The chaste snow, which gave so agreeable a covering to the ice, was now no more to be seen; a dirty forbidding surface became its substitute, and those objects which I had so long looked upon with unceasing delight, were now, from the loss of their modest clothing, offensive to the eye.

The ship being nearly at rest, Captain Scoresby made some curious experiments to exhibit the effect of the pressure of the water, at given depths, in the following manner: a glass quart bottle was closely stopped with a piece of very dry close-grained wood, about three inches in length, and extremely buoyant; the bottle was then weighed with the greatest exactness, and by means of a deep sea lead, it was lowered 250 yards into the sea; after remaining down some time it was hauled up, and it was found that the pressure of the water upon the stopper, had forced that fluid through the pores of the wood, and that the bottle had received two ounces of sea-water. The bottle was in a like manner prepared for a second experiment, and lowered to the depth of 1,000 yards, but the immense pressure of the volume of water at that depth had broken the bottle. The wooden stopper was next examined; it had not only lost its original buoyancy, but acquired a ponderous nature; it sank like a stone, and was found to have increased by one half of its original weight; on splitting it, the pores shewed that they had all been conductors of the fluid. To extend this interesting experiment, I furnished Captain Scoresby with a strong oblong copper vessel, in the mouth of which a long piece of wood was securely screwed, so as to prevent a possibility of any water entering; and it was sunk nearly to the depth of one mile. On bringing it up, the enormous pressure to which it had been subjected was found to have crushed the vessel into the most irregular form, and forced the upper side into the lower. The estimated load of pressure was fifty tons, being equal to a ton upon a square inch.

Having seen several seals of late, many of which I had shot, but lost them, as they sank the moment they were killed, I was induced to try another experiment, particularly on seeing a handsome young one which I was desirous to get; I, therefore, instead of shooting it with a ball through its head, fired a charge of small shot into its nose; it sank as I expected, but soon returned to the surface perfectly stunned, and with ease I thus procured it.

August 6. The fog having continued extremely thick all yesterday, and our progress being still interrupted by large floes of ice, which required all possible precaution to avoid, we did not advance far. The great prevalence of foggy weather to which these seas are subject, unquestionably arises, as Captain Scoresby considers, from the damp air near the surface of the sea, being chilled by coming in contact with the ice; and it is singularly curious, that the fog frequently rests on the surface, not far exceeding the height of the ship's upper masts, while the sky above is perfectly clear. Just at midday the horizon began to be clear, and the sea stream of ice became visible from the mast-head.

As the wind blew hard, directly towards the body of ice, much minute observation was required in approaching it; for several miles within the range of sight, large fragments of ice were scattered in every direction; among these, the ship was steered in a masterly manner, to avoid the many obstacles that in this intricate navigation prevented our keeping a direct course. At length an opening was observed, when having passed through it, we bade adieu to the comforts of smooth water, which we had enjoyed while we were among the ice: and I expected the turbulence of the ocean would again bring back the horrible sufferings of sea-sickness, which I so severely experienced at the commencement of the voyage. We sailed to the southward, to look for whales in that quarter, and I went to my cabin, in the hope of averting those feelings which I was confident a most raging sea would cause to return.

August 10. At two o'clock in the morning it was announced to me that the island of Jan Mayne was in sight, on which I arose, and saw the east side of it. It presented nothing unusual to the general appearance of distant land. It was much obscured in a mist, and only a part rising from the margin of the ocean was visible; but as we approached it, new objects presented themselves and kept the attention continually alive. About five o'clock, the sun, which had not, during the last fortnight, shed its kind rays upon us, indicated a disposition to re-appear; a circumstance most important to us, as a means of taking observations, as well as gratifying to nature by the animation which its presence imparts. As the mist rapidly dispersed the land soon presented its variegated and richly stratified cliff to our view: over the face of which lofty boundary, in extensive recesses from the summit, the three celebrated icebergs were united. These polar glaciers, created by the melting of the snow under the summer sun, being annually increased by the frozen severity of winter, were sublimely grand; they were upwards of 1,200 feet in altitude, and resembled immense cataracts curving to the form of the cliffs, over which they passed; while patches of snow, not unlike foam, gave a pleasing variety to the dark front of rock to which they were united by frozen ties; and ridges of the same attracted the attention by the relief they bestowed upon this sterile boundary. Just as we arrived at the south point, the sun had acquired power to disperse the misty vapour that was mantling the brow of the cliff, and in a short time it withdrew its fleecy curtain, and unfolded to our sight, the magnificent and lofty mountain of Beeringberg, or Bear's Mountain, which from its extraordinary steepness, can only be accessible to these lords of the soil. To say that I was lost in astonishment, on beholding this wonderful promontory, is saying too little, for language cannot express my feelings, on beholding the transition produced in one minute by the vanishing of a dense fog. Part of this colossal feature was exhibited,

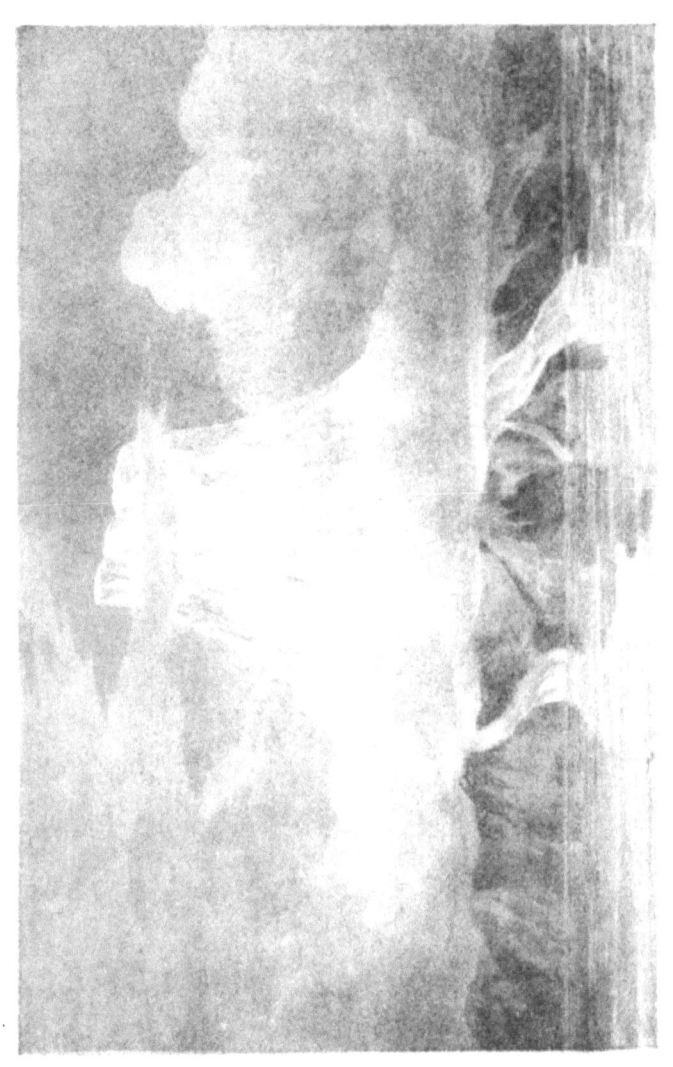

BERENGBERG FROM N.E OF JAN MAYEN.
With 2 of the Icebergs

London. Pub by G. & W. B. Whittaker Ave Maria Lane

rising in the most graceful form in a clear and cheerful atmosphere: it was clad in the whitest snow; a rich cloud concealed a narrow space just below its summit, and a few patches of dark protruding rock, which, from their position, did not afford a rest for the snow, gave a pleasing variety to the extensive mass of white; these appeared to be of the darkest blue colour, not probably from the hue of the stone, but from the tint given by distance; a curtain of mist, in a direct line, took from my sight the pedestal and base of this elevated mountain, and formed a relief to the dark boundary of the cliff.

The south-west side of the island appeared to be volcanic, and on observation the relics of a crater became discernible. From the south-west end, a most abrupt termination arrested my attention. It appeared to be unlike the rock that formed the other part of the boundary of the island, and seemed as though it had been disjointed from the cliff by some extraordinary convulsion of nature. If ever there had been a continuity from this island to that of Iceland, here was unquestionably its course; and it is an extraordinary coincidence, that this apparently disjointed part was in the direct line to that island. The surface of Jan Mayne that came under my view had but little snow upon it, and that only in small patches, drifted into hollows; the rest of the soil had an unvaried covering of short herbage like grass. The wind blowing a very fresh breeze, accompanied by those dangerous squalls so usual near this island, we were prevented from going on shore, which I anxiously desired, with the view of collecting subjects of natural history, specimens of mineralogy and of volcanic productions; and also to have some excellent shooting. Many birds indeed were seen from the ship, particularly the *Alca Arctica*, or Greenland parrot, one of which I succeeded in shooting, as numbers of them flew round the vessel, the representation of which is herewith given.

Beeringberg exhibited its towering head continually during the brightness of the day, until it gradually sank into the ocean when we had left the island upwards of eighty miles behind us. Captain Scoresby availed himself of the clearness of the weather to survey the south and west sides of the island, and took some observations highly important to navigation; for he discovered an error in the charts, the situation of Jan Mayne being laid down upwards of two degrees of longitude, and from ten to fifteen miles of latitude, from its real position. He also took the altitude of its stupendous mountain geometrically, and found it to be six thousand eight hundred and seventy feet above the level of the sea. As we proceeded along the south and west sides, we sounded in thirty-seven fathoms, and brought up small shells. In the early part of the season the ice not only often surrounds this island, but extends from hence to the east side of Old Greenland. This island derives its name from that of a Dutch navigator who first saw it, in 1611; soon after that period it was visited by some whale fishers from Hull, who named it Trinity Island, and it was, on the petition of the corporation of that port, granted to them by King James 1st. It lies between 70° 50′, and 71° 8′ north latitude, and between 7° 26′, and 8° 44′ west longitude. It is in length about ten leagues north-east and south-west, and does not exceed three leagues in breadth over any part. The northern extremity is of a rhomboidal form, where the remarkable peak or mountain of Beeringberg is seated, the base of which covers the width; but the southern extremity of the island does not exceed three or four miles in width. The Dutch, from deriving great advantage by the practice, constantly visited this island from its earliest discovery, for the purpose of fishing; and in 1633, seven seamen of that nation made the attempt to pass the winter there, no doubt, with a view of establishing a colony, but they masked their scheme, under the pretence of determining some scientific observations disputed among astronomers. It appears, that they survived the winter's severity, but fell a sacrifice to the effects of scurvy; for, on the island being visited in the following summer, their dead bodies were found in their huts. A journal was discovered which they had kept from August the 26th, until April the 31st, and it was therefore supposed, that the last died about that time, as it contains some interesting remarks on the state of the wind, a copy of which is given by Churchill as follows:

STATE OF THE WIND AND WEATHER, FROM AUGUST TO MAY, IN THE ISLAND OF JAN MAYEN, AS COLLECTED FROM THE JOURNAL OF SEVEN SAILORS OF HOLLAND WHO WINTERED THERE IN THE YEAR 1633-4.

1633.		Winds.	Remarks.
Aug.	26	NE	Strong breeze. The fleet sailed for Holland
	27	NE	
	28	NE	Snow
	29		Clear
	30	NW, at night NE	
	31	NE	Fresh gale, clear
Sept.	1	NW to NE	Snow
	2	NE	Snow
	3	NE	Some snow
	4	NE	Some snow
	5	NE	Some snow
	6	NE	Rainy
	7	NE	Fair. At night SEbS rainy
	8	SE	Rainy Morning
	9	SE	Clear and warm
	10	SE	Very stormy, rainy
	11	SEbS to SW and NE	Foggy, rainy
	12	NE	Blowing hard, clear

| 1633. | Winds. | Remarks. |

Sept. 13 SE to NEbN and NW. Fair, sun-shiny
    14 W, NWbW Some snow
    15 W Blowing so hard the sea foamed
    16 SW Fair
    17 SW Blowing very hard, clear
    18 SWbS Rainy
    19 W,SE Clear, starlight at night
    20 SEbS,SW Sunshiny
    21 SW Misty and rainy
    22 SW Blowing hard and rainy
    23 EbSE Cloudy, with rain and mist
    24 SEbS Rainy
    25 SEbE Stormy and rainy
    26 E.erly Frosty weather
    27 NE Fair, at night W Foul weather
    28 N,S,SE Violent storm, snow
    29 SE Blowing hard, with snow
    30 SWbW Rainy, stormy at night
Oct. 1 NE Frosty
    2 E Freezing hard
    3 E,W Frost and snow
    4 S,SW Frosty, fog or rain at night
    5 SW Much rain
    6 SWbS Blowing hard
    7 SWbW Very stormy
    8 SWbW, NE, E Very tempestuous
    9 N.erly Tempestuous
    10 NEbN Blowing strong, excessive cold
    11 NE Very cold, snow
    12 NE Blowing hard, very cold
    13 NE Very cold
    14 NE Excessive cold
    15 N.erly Weather tolerable
    16 N.erly Cold, snow
    17 N Blowing hard, frosty
    18 N Frosty

1632.	Winds.	Remarks.
Oct. 19	N	Some *ice* a mile off shore
20	NE	Fair, much ice seen
21	E,NE	Blowing and snowing hard
22	NE	Much snow
23	NE	Cloudy
24	NE	Frosty
25	SW	Excessive cold, clear
26	SW, W	Sea full of ice
27	W	Clear
28	W	Clear frosty weather
29	N	Severe cold, sea full of ice, snow
30	N	Freezing hard, tempestuous
31	N	Severe frost, with snow
Nov. 1	NE	Cold vehement
2		Hard frost
3	NE	Tolerable weather
4	NE, W	Freezing hard
5	S	Heavy fall of snow
6	S to E	Tempestuous weather
7	NE	Still weather.
8	N	Excessive cold
9	N	Sun ½ an hour above the horizon
10	N	
11	NE	Wind increased, thick clouds
12	E	Thick fogs, gulls seen
13	E	Freezing severely
14	E, W	Cold weather, bay full of ice
15	W	Saw three or four bears
16	W	
17	N	Dark snowy weather, cold relaxed
18	NE	Frost increased
19	N	Sun seen just above the sea
20	N, W	Dark snowy weather
21	W	Sea full of ice
22	W.erly	Cold weather
23	NWbN	Fair, sea full of ice

| 1633. | Winds. | Remarks. |

Nov. 24 SE, W Frosty, sea gulls seen
25 W Frosty
26 S Mild, the ice left the bay
27 SW, E Fair weather
28 SE Fair mild weather
29 SE Land blocked with ice on S side
30 SE Violent rains

Dec. 1 S.erly Rain, SE at night
2 SE Mild rainy wr. ice set off the land
3 S Rainy, blowing strong
4 S Mild, cloudy
5 S Mild calm weather
6 SE Cloudy
7 SE,S Foggy, snow and frost
8 NE, W Frosty
9 W Clear cold weather, sea full of ice
10 W Frosty nothing but ice at sea
11 W Ditto
12 W Cold weather, calm at night
13 SW Cloudy, SE at night with snow
14 S Clear frosty day, ice removed off land
15 S Dark wr. ice returned
16 SW Moonlight night
17 S Cloudy dark wr. snow, thaw at night
18 S, E Dark rainy day
19 E Hard frost
20 E Do. calm weather dark night
21 E, N Frost and snow
22 N Ice returned, coldest day yet experienced
23 E Frost, snow, stormy night
24 E, NE Hard frost and storm at night
25 S Fair day, at night wind N
26 E, NW Clear frosty day
27 NW At night calm, wind E.erly
28 E, W Violent snow and wind
29 W Clear cold wr. SE at nt. with snow

1633.	Winds.	Remarks.
30	SW	Blowing hard
31	SW	Calm, snow at night

1634
Jan.
1 SW Dark cold weather
2 NE Clear, ice forced to sea
3 SE, A little rain, at night a SW storm
4 W.erly Fierce wind, cold weather, ice returned; E.erly wind at night

Jan. 5 E.erly Thick fog and frost
6 N Increasing wind, with snow
7 N Snowing and freezing hard
8 NE Frosty, excessive cold and stormy at night
9 NE The ice heaped in the bay like huts
10 NE Bright pleasant day, but very cold
11 NE to S & SE Vast quantity of snow with SE wind
12 SE Vast quantity of sn. fell, wr. milder
13 SE Do., ice forced to sea, cold wr.
14 E Tolerably clear
15 E.erly, NE. Snow, ice seen off shore
16 S Milder wr. E at night, with frost
17 E Fog, N at night, froze the bay up in a night
18 N to W Cold, foggy, snow
19 W Abundance of snow
20 W.erly Much snow, E at night, snow
21 E Blowing violently, with thick snow, W at night
22 W A heavy fall of snow
23 W to E Sun visible, clear frosty wr. ice went off
24 W Snowy, S wind at night, cloudy
25 S Strong wind, cold night
26 W Snowing hrd. ice returned, S at night
27 W Mild, E at night, snowy weather
28 W to SE Snow, ice carried a great way off
29 SW, W Dark rainy wr. ice returned
30 Calm clear frosty day, sun seen an hour and a half
31 W.erly, N with frost

| 1634. | Winds. | Remarks. |

Feb. 1 W.erly Clear calm wr., bay full of ice
2 NE Clear cold wr. bears grow shy
3 E.erly, SE Cloudy, milder
4 SE to S Milder, snow, ice went off
5 SE and E Cold abated
6 E to SW Clear moonlight night
7 E Blowing strong
8 S Calm wr., ice was carried out of sight
9 N.erly Snowed violently; at night S
10 N to SW Dark and stormy
11 S to E Cloudy
12 E Snow; not very cold for the season
13 E Snowy, calm wr. moonlight night
14 E Clear day; stormy cloudy night
15 E Snow so high could not stir out
16 E Mild, saw two fowls like geese and a falcon
17 E Much snow
18 E Cloudy, mild weather
19 E Fair day, no ice
20 E Mild weather
21 NE Fair and calm, frost and snow at night
22 NE Much snow, frosty
23 NE Some ice returned to the bay
24 E.erly Intense frost, N at night
25 N Cloudy dark night
26 (No remark)
27 Calm mild weather, S wind at night and thaw
28 S Mild wr. ice far off, SW at night

March 1 SW Rainy in the evening
2 W Blowing hard, clear cold weather
3 NE to N Violent wind forced the ice into the bay
4 NE Cloudy calm weather
5 NE Cloudy, cold less severe
6 NE Pleasant, and calm at night
7 NE Do. at night stormy
8 NE Dark cloudy weather

1634.	Winds.	Remarks.
Mar. 9	NE	Sharp frost
10	NE	Excessive cold weather
11	NE	A south wind brought pleasant wr.
12	S, SE	Ice went out of sight, do. wr.
13	SE NE	Moderately cold
14	NE	Very cold
15	S, SW	Milder wr. killed a bear, which was very serviceable, as the scurvy had appeared
16	SW, N	At night, cold weather
17	N	Cloudy, bay filled with ice
18	N	Cloudy frosty day
19		(No remark)
20	S	Calm, sunshiny day
21	S	Dark rainy weather, ice went to sea
22	SE	Scurvy becomes very afflictive
23	SE	Pleasant day
24	S.erly	or calm weather
25	SE, S	Ice returned
26	S	Fair clear weather
27	SE	Cloudy, 10 whales seen in the bay
28	S.erly	wind innumerable whales appeared
29	S.erly	Plenty of whales
30	S.erly	Dark night
31	NE	Some snow, 4 or 5 whales seen
April 1	E	Cloudy, S at night, 4 or 5 whales
2	SE	Snow, mild weather
3	W	Cloudy, two of the men only in health
4	W erly	sunshiny day
5	SE	Two large whales in the bay
6	NE	4 or 5 whales
7	NE	Cold, sunshiny weather
8	NE	Do. innumerable whales
9	N	Frosty, do.
10	N	Cold, ice returned, some whales
11	N	No whales or bears
12	NE	Clear frosty day

| 1634. | Winds. | Remarks. |

April 13 NE Do. bay full of ice
    14 NE, A south wind at night carried the ice away
    15 W Calm mild day, 4 whales seen in the bay
    16 W Clear. *The clerk died*
    17 W Cloudy, bay full of ice
    18 (No remark)
    19 W The men much afflicted, having no refreshment left
    20 S At night E.erly, with snow ; ice drifted away
    21 SE A calm day
    22 NE Ice closed to the shore ; S wind at night
    23 S Ice off land, rain. All the survivors but one rendered helpless by disease; the captain struggling with death
    24 S Cloudy
    25 S Sunshiny, some ice whales seen ; A W wind at night brought the ice in
    26 W Cloudy day, calm
    27 E Mild weather, killed a dog for food
    28 E Cloudy weather, ice went out of sight, N wind at night
    29 NE Blowing hard at night
    30 NE A fine clear day

Here the journal terminates with the word *die*; alluding perhaps to other observations which the writer in his usual way had been about to set down. The first man of this unfortunate party died on the 16th of April, the other six seem to have expired in the beginning of May. The scurvy was evidently the cause of their death, which, it appears, arose more from the want of fresh provisions than from the cold, as they could generally stir abroad at least once in three or four days.

We found that the ice had now totally disappeared, and as we observed neither whales, nor appearances indicating a probability of finding any in this quarter, we sailed to the north-west with a strong breeze, and saw a large tree at sea, for which we lay to; when it was hoisted on board, it proved to be the lower part of a fir, without branches or bark, twenty-five feet in length, and four feet in girth; it had been felled by fire, as is usual in some parts of America, to clear the ground, and it bore the marks of having long contended with ice and the elements. The distinction between day and night now began to be apparent, and the splendid luminary was again seen by us to take its diurnal farewell, sinking below the horizon at twenty minutes past ten o'clock.

August 12. We continued our course to the north-west, until we met with ice, which from the return of fog, compelled us to steer to the south-west. It was His Majesty's birth-day, but being Sunday, we contented ourselves with drinking our sovereign's health in heart-felt loyalty. On the 13th, however, we resolved to celebrate the event, which we should have commemorated on the preceding day, by a repast, probably different from that of any of our fellow subjects. Our feast was on a leg of mutton that we had brought out with us and which had been suspended under the mizen-top for a hundred and thirty-one days; it was full of gravy, and as fine flavoured as ever was eaten: such a repast heightened the joys of the day, and we drank with glee, a long, happy, and glorious reign to our King, and prosperity to our country; nor did we forget our wives and friends at home.

August 14. On this, and the two following days, an inveterate fog, attended with rain and a heavy gale of wind, perplexed us, and called forth every precaution that prudence could dictate to preserve us from danger, as nothing warned us of our approach to the ice, but the hideous dashing of the waves against its rugged borders. Repeatedly did detached pieces strike the ship with a degree of violence, that made our situation fearful, and often, as far as our limited sight would allow, we beheld heavy pieces in every direction. In this state of anxiety we passed three days; our progress was almost totally impeded, and to add to our apprehensions, the nights were now become extremely dark.

August 17. At four o'clock the fog began to disperse, and we found ourselves by the side of a long and heaving stream of ice, running east and west; the pieces composing it were violently agitated by a lofty swell, that rendered it too hazardous to attempt passing through it; we therefore sailed in a westerly direction by the side of it, for upwards of fifteen miles. This long tract of connected ice, is one of those peculiarities which render the navigation of an arctic sea so very difficult, that the skilful accomplishment of it can only be attained by much experience. The ice that we this day saw much resembled what we had met with during the voyage, being branches in the form of the fingers of the hand widely distended, extending from the great mass of western ice, to a distance of perhaps from fifty to a hundred miles. Should a ship unfortunately go with a fair wind into one of these bights, the difficulty of getting out again must be obvious, and it is from this consideration that the commanders of whale ships invariably keep beating to windward, particularly in thick weather; the better to be enabled in cases of entanglement, to avail themselves of a leading wind to ensure their return to safety. I was here struck with the singular character and appearance of the ice; the heavy rains and the dense fogs, that had so long prevailed, had entirely dissolved the snow from its surface, and it was apparent that the lashings of the sea had made considerable ravages upon it. Its opaqueness intimated that it had received its origin from sea water, and in those recesses where shadows were created, were tints, whose richness not only emulated but excelled the sapphire in lustre. The effect of the waves upon the elevated pieces, explained the manner in which the beautiful and graceful forms assumed by the ice were modelled; and proved that it was the continual action of the water, which produced that evenness of surface, and formed those elegant tablets and other figures, so distinguished for correctness of proportion; it was also observable, that it was to the washing of the sea, the height of which limited the length of the stems of ice, that their tasteful forms were to be ascribed.

At this period of the year, the mildness of the temperature permits the specimens thus manufactured to possess but little durability. The shafts rapidly decrease in size, until unable to support their elegant summits, they sink beneath the graceful load. About six o'clock we cleared the stream, and came into an ocean thickly strewed with small pieces of ice, in every fanciful variety of shape, reflecting a multitude of colours from the sun-beams; and calculated to recall to the mind, descriptions of the enchanted castles of romance. Before dark, we got into a clear though turbulent sea, to the infinite joy of all who preferred safety to comfort, and sailed to the south-west, with the design as Captain Scoresby stated, of again entering the ice in search of whales in a southern direction, a circumstance that gave me much gratification, in the hope that an opportunity might still be afforded, for the crew to benefit those interested in the concerns of the ship. Captain Scoresby also intimated his intention to examine the ice in the parallel of Iceland, and in this unexplored region (where, if there were any whales, they would be undisturbed and easy of capture), to endeavour to make up for that deficiency of success, which he had experienced in the more northern stations. As the ice is supposed usually to lie altogether to the westward of Iceland, there was a probability that we should get within sight of West Greenland, and proceed homeward by the strait between Iceland and Greenland. As our coals were nearly expended, there was also a great chance of our being obliged to land in Iceland, to replenish our fuel. This communication afforded me considerable satisfaction, as it would enable me to accomplish the strong wish which I had formed, of visiting a country so distinguished for its celebrated volcanoes and basaltic pillars. I longed to examine, on the spot, the tremendous effects which are there produced upon the surface of the ground, by the contention of the elements beneath its foundations, and to behold those scenes unrivalled in nature, where lofty columns of boiling water are jetted from caldrons heated by subterraneous fires; my object was also in some measure to witness the happiness of a race of people, who, although living in a most remote country under the greatest privations, are so warmly attached to their native land, that they rank themselves among the most blessed people of the earth; and agree with their old proverb that; *Istand on hinn besta land sem solinn skinnar uppa,* "Iceland is the best land on which the sun shines." This simple race afford a fine moral lesson to every country, and a censure on those dissatisfied creatures, who are living in the land of liberty, gifted with the bounties of Providence, even the choicest fruits of the earth, and who yet are not contented.

The island of Iceland had the honour of giving birth to the discoverer of Old Greenland. Eric Rande, or, Eric the Red, (so called from the colour of his hair), about the year 892, set sail from Snafaldes on an expedition to the westward, and fell in with a point of land called Herjolf's Ness. Sailing to the south, he then entered a large inlet, which was thenceforth named Eric's Sound. Here he landed to spend the winter, and having explored the coast, returned to Iceland, where he gave so favourable a description of its green and pleasant meadows, (from which it obtained the name of Greenland), that many persons were induced to colonize it. About the year 1000, Christianity began to flourish in the new settlement; a cathedral and several churches were built along the coast, and the bishop's residence established at Gardé, a little to the south of the polar circle. At a small place called Albe, a monastery was also founded near a volcano, the subterraneous fire of which causing a spring of boiling water to rise, the fluid was conducted in that state into the houses of this religious fraternity for all culinary purposes. Many public buildings were also erected in the colony, which, for a few centuries, proceeded prosperously, until it was visited by the dreadful pestilence, termed *the black death*, which commenced its fatal career in Cathay or China in 1346; spread all over Asia and Africa, and reaching to the south of Europe in 1347, extended itself in the following year to Britain, Germany, the north of Europe Iceland, and finally to this unfortunate colony Since this period of calamity, the settlement has been little heard of, and never even visited, to discover whether the whole of the inhabitants perished, or whether any of the ancient race are remaining. That this country, however, is still able to support a colony, may appear from the following considerations. The island of Iceland is exactly in the same latitude, as that part of Greenland to which I refer. It is represented by Mr. Henderson, who has recently visited it, as being capable of growing corn, but the inhabitants consider the cultivation of grass, for the benefit of breeding sheep, to be more to their advantage. The numerous lakes, rivers and streams which intersect the island, produce an extraordinary abundance of salmon, and salmon trout; and, on the coast, cod and other sea fish are in profusion; birds for the sustenance and comfort of man are also found in the greatest plenty, and turf for fuel to supply all possible wants. I cannot therefore suppose that the same bounties of a kind Providence, would be withheld from Greenland, a country so nearly and similarly situated. I wish now to refer my reader to the general map, and to call his attention to the west side, or opposite coast of Old Greenland, (running by the side of Davis' Straits), for the purpose of shewing in what high latitudes that part is inhabited, and that, consequently, the colonization of the eastern side would have nothing of peculiar severity in it. The west side of Old Greenland was visited and minutely examined, in the year 1813, by Sir Charles Giesecke, and divided into two districts; from Cape Farewell, or the southern extremity, to Ice-blink were two thousand three hundred and fourteen souls; and from

Ice-blink to the north-east of Baal's river, seven hundred and sixty-nine more. At this last point the southern district terminated; and the northern commencing here, extended to latitude 76° 3' N. It contained the following divisions; Eges-mindes, Christian-haab, Jacob's-haun, Ormenisks, and Upperville; and possessed a population of three thousand persons. The country from Lat. 67° to 69° is inhabited; the natives belonging to this division situated round Disco, or fish bay, have their houses at these colonies for the sake of the whale fishery. The natives of Ormenisks live in the interior during winter for the convenience of catching seals. At Tessarereist, an island in 74° 15', resides one family who are the most northern inhabitants known. The southern part of Old Greenland, as laid down in the ancient Dutch charts, is intersected by three pervious straits or passages, stretching across the country from the east coast to that of Davis' Straits; these are laid down as follows: the most southerly is at Ice-blink, and this channel is presumed to be the strait in which Frobisher penetrated sixty leagues in 1576, and to which his name was given. At the western entrance of this inlet, is said to be one of the most extraordinary phenomena ever beheld; in an arched bridge formed of ice, extending from land to land, for the space of eight leagues in length and two in breadth. The next passage is represented to be about thirty-two leagues further to the north, at Bar or Bear sound; and the last opens from Ice bay, Disco.

In making these observations my purpose has been to excite an interest on the subject of Old or lost Greenland; and to induce an attempt towards its recovery. A voyage to this colony might, unless the interposition of ice or foul winds should prevent it, be made in ten days; the expenses therefore attendant on a discovery of that part, from the southern extremity to the polar circle, would be comparatively small, and probably it might be effected by holding out a premium to masters of whale ships, for the best survey and description of the coast; for I have been informed, that some ships had it in their power, during last season, to have effected a landing without difficulty or even hazard.

August 21. A strong gale of wind, the thickest fog possible, and the most turbulent sea I ever experienced, with the rugged shore of Iceland partly under our lee, placed us in much anxiety and peril, as our reckoning brought us within a few miles of the land, and all who were conversant with navigation judged that we were about to be drawn into one of the bights of the island. Ice was also seen, and found to extend at least two hundred miles to the eastward of its ordinary course, and in a position extremely unfavourable, as well as perilous to fishing. These multiplied obstructions and dangers changed the intention of our cautious and experienced commander, who, for the safety of the ship, deemed it prudent to bear up, in order to avoid the land and the ice. All hopes of further success in the fishing were now at an end, as perseverance would only be attended with danger and needless expenses; so our course was directed for England, from the following causes, as they were expressed in the Captain's log. " The incessant prevalence of fog, the increased darkness of the nights, the prevailing tempestuous weather, and the occurrence of ice to the eastward of Langaness, were circumstances which combined to render the prosecution of my design for trying for whales, on the west coast of Iceland, not merely hazardous, but impracticable. I had entertained considerable hopes of the result of an examination of this unfrequented and undisturbed sea; especially as in our advance to the southward, we passed several patches of great extent of turbid water, and of a quality very congenial to the habits and feeding of the whale. The fog, which we in a degree calculated on, would have been a great difficulty to contend with; but the occurrence of ice being now unexpected, was an additional difficulty, and of such a nature as to leave no hope of our succeeding, except at a risk which the prospect of success would by no means warrant. The sea, about Iceland, is at this season, I believe, almost invariably free from ice, even on the N. W. part, where its approach is nearest. The circumstance of its now lying so far to the eastward must, therefore, be extremely rare. During the forty-one days preceding this, we had but three clear days, with two or three more of slightly hazy weather: and, for many successive days, we had not a clear moment, and sometimes the farthest we could see throughout the day was a mile or two, at others not two hundred yards, and very often the intensity of the mist was such, that a mass of ice could not be discerned at the distance of fifty yards: yet, amidst this universal obscurity we passed in direct lines, (not reckoning the stretches in tacking) six or seven hundred miles through immense fields, floes, and crowded drift ice, and traced, as well as possible for the time, the edge of the ice next the sea, a distance of five or six hundred miles more. We sailed above twice that distance in search of fish, throughout their most usual and favourite haunts, but saw very few. And from the west land in Lat. $74\frac{1}{2}$ Long. 14 W., to the sea edge in 1 W. in the same parallel, and from thence down to our quitting the fishing sea, we never saw a single whale. As I could not feel myself justified in persevering to the westward under such untoward circumstances, I determined very reluctantly to abandon further pursuit, notwithstanding our indifferent cargo, and to proceed homeward; steering therefore S.S.E. to give a birth to the ice, and the land during the fog, we took leave of the ice at a period twenty days later than I had ever before been amidst these evidences of the irresistible bonds of frost."

The occurrences of our voyage, after we left the ice, were of continued sameness, too trivial to be either worthy of observation or amusing; they may be thus briefly related: an uninterrupted series of most unfavourable weather conspired to try our patience; for nine successive days, it blew with the greatest violence, and without intermission, (often attended with heavy rain) directly in opposition to us, by which we were driven upwards of three hundred miles, not only out of our course, but into the horribly agitated Atlantic Ocean.

Sept. 3. With a delight beyond the power of words to express, we at day-break, saw the north end of Ireland; the wind blowing a gale prevented our ascertaining with correctness, what part it was; consequently we kept sailing on and off with great caution, to avert the perils attendant on a stormy night, and the dangers of the coast.

Sept. 4. Finding it impossible to keep our course, on account of the adverse wind, and the extreme violence with which it blew, we endeavoured, towards dark, to seek shelter under the lee of Rachlin Island, very thick weather having set in.

Sept. 5. The light of the day appearing, we endeavoured to proceed on our course, though the fog was so thick, that we could not see three hundred yards from the ship. At six o'clock the curtain of this immense vapour was withdrawn, and unfolded the lofty promontory of Fair Head, so beautifully distinguished by the noble basaltic columns that adorn its brow, and render it one of the boldest and most picturesque headlands imaginable. The sun had now begun partially to shine upon the coast, and to cheer us with its delightful rays as we passed along; embellishing the fertilized land, and gilding the little patches of yellow corn, scattered over the face of the mountains. After having so long witnessed the dreary and desolate prospect of ice and snow, unrelieved by the sight of a single habitation, the enchanting picture of verdant hills studded with earth, of luxuriant corn fields, waving with the weight of the bounties of Providence, and of the peaceful abodes of civilization, produced a pleasure of which it would be vain to attempt a description. This pleasing view attended us while we sailed along the coast, and until the frightful appearance of rocks and breakers, warning us of hidden dangers, bade us keep further aloof from the land. These rocks are called the Maidens; and in their faithless arms many a sailor has miserably perished.

The wind now changing to the S.S.W., began to blow a hurricane, and every effort was made to weather the much dreaded rocks, called the Chickens, projecting from the south of the Isle of Man, but all in vain; and we were obliged to beat between that island and Ireland, during one of the most dismal nights ever experienced; in the course of which we were, by a change of wind, blown nearly into one of the bights of the Irish coast, where we must inevitably have perished. We also narrowly escaped being run down by a large ship, which, in the extreme darkness that prevailed, was scudding before the gale.

Sept. 6. The gale continued all the day with a fury, unequalled during the voyage, which, with a lofty tumbling swell, drove us to leeward in spite of a pressure of sail, that kept the ship upon her beam ends.

Sept. 7. The gale moderated in the morning, but the head swell prevented our weathering the Calf of Man until the evening, when the wind changing a few points to the westward, enabled us to proceed some distance beyond that dangerous promontory, before the sun's golden orb had sunk into its watery bed. Never did I behold departing day retire more slowly and beautifully, and I could not help hailing it as a welcome to our return, and a reproach as it were, to the elements that had used their unkind influence to retard our progress, ever since our ship's head had been turned towards home.

Sept. 8. At day-light I heard this joyful sound vociferated; " land right ahead;" and before it could be distinctly seen I was on the deck, and soon after heard it pronounced to be Great Ormes head, on the coast of Wales. It assumed the character of a most sterile cliff of considerable elevation, and appeared as barren a spot as nature ever formed; but to behold any part of our country, gives a joy to the heart which is impossible to be described, and affords to the eyes, a sight most gladdening and refreshing after the continued appearance of ice, snow, and water.

To behold our native land, always excites the tenderest emotions on the mind, yet, the anticipated pleasure receives a chill, from the dreaded apprehension of hearing of the death of some much regarded friend, or, some fatality to our country, and it is this circumstance, which renders a voyage to Greenland so particularly distressing, as no possibility presents itself of the least intelligence until the return. The first gleam of sun as far as the eye could reach, was shining over a country; the mountain-tops of which were obscured in clouds, and extending its brilliancy over a varied tract covered with the charms of luxuriant vegetation, and of picturesque fertility. At eleven o'clock in the forenoon, we took in a pilot, from whom we heard the particular occurrences that had interested the nation during our absence. On the ship's private ensign being displayed at six o'clock in the evening, we saw the signal station on the Cheshire hills announcing our approach, and in two hours after, on account of the tide, we anchored off Black Rock. Our anchor had not long received its welcome in English soil before boats came conveying friends, deeply interested in our safety and success, to greet our return.

Our expedition being now at an end, I must add one word more to upbraid Fortune for her unkindness, in not rewarding those spirited speculators who were our ship's owners, and repaying the exertions of the crew with better success. I must also reproach her in not affording me an opportunity of practically trying the value of improvements in the whale fishery, which were designed to *produce confidence, dispel prejudice,* encourage exertion, and to excite in the mind of those at present indifferent to the proposed changes, that degree of zeal, on which may be placed the most cheerful assurance of the certainty of success, when it is properly applied.

My situation and experience will justify one other remark; never was there a more vigilant, indefatigable, and zealous officer, than the distinguished arctic navigator, who commanded the Baffin; never one who has had so much practical experience in the navigation of ice; or, perhaps, in whom were united those various philosophical and scientific talents, essentially requisite for success in attempting discoveries hitherto prevented by a frozen boundary. I feel the most confident persuasion, that should Captain Scoresby ever be selected for public service, he would prove himself an ornament to his profession, and an honour to his country.

Not having been on shore for twenty-two weeks, I availed myself, as may be supposed, of the first boat that left the ship, and it was not without the warmest feelings of a grateful heart to the goodness of Providence, that I again set my foot upon my native land; for my health and age had been considered by my friends to be incompatible with so arduous an undertaking.

END OF THE JOURNAL.

APPENDIX.

APPENDIX.

Remarks upon the Failure which has for some Years attended the Whale-Fishery; with Considerations for removing the Obstacles which have occasioned the same.

OF the importance of the *Greenland Fishery*, in its direct objects of procuring an article of great profit to the nation; and, collaterally, as a nursery of seamen for our navy, there can be no doubt. But the fishery is now carried on by individuals at very extraordinary and increased expense, while the late *frequent failures*, the losses of ships crushed among the ice, and, above all, the vast reduction in the price of oil, owing to the substitution of coal gas to light this metropolis*, have considerably dispirited enterprise. It is evident, that a continuance of such failures alone, without other casualties to which the speculation is liable, may quite extinguish adventure, and, finally, deprive the nation of the advantages of the northern whale fishery.

The failures of late seasons have principally arisen

---

* The advantage of gas produced from oil, compared with that obtained from coal, is so great that it is astonishing that oil gas is not in general use. The gas from oil has no bad nor disagreeable quality, it gives a far more brilliant light than the other, " one cubic foot of gas from oil, going as far as twice that quantity of coal gas," and it is moreover much cheaper. That from coal on the contrary, is extremely offensive to the smell, dangerous to the health on being inhaled; and injurious to furniture, books, plate, pictures, &c.

from the increased difficulty of taking whales. Formerly, in the early and flourishing state of the fishery, the fish were found in bays, and open water, numerous, unwary, very accessible, and easily taken by the methods first practised, and still in use. But the increased numbers of ships fitted out in this branch of commerce, have not only diminished the quantity of fish, but greatly added to the annoyance of those yet remaining; the perpetual alarm to which the whales are now exposed, has caused them to abandon their former favourite haunts, for places of greater security. Whales are naturally timid, and they have from repeated attacks, also become more shy, (many from ineffectual wounds by harpoons which have not held,) so that the fish are now but rarely to be approached close enough to be struck by the harpoon from the hand.

The hand harpoon is thus constructed:

It consists of three conjoined parts, denominated the socket, shank, and mouth; the latter including the pointed arms, termed the withers, which are six inches distant from each other. This implement can, of course, be used only at a very short distance from the fish; and the unaided power of the arm, however close to the object, is always insufficient to pierce the prey to a vital part; but, if the harpoon be *thrown* at a fish, the impetus is then often inadequate to penetrate even to those parts, which afford sufficient hold to the harpoon to resist the powerful efforts of the fish to extricate itself; in this case, the retraction of the harpoon is almost of certain occurrence.

It will be observed, that the arms or withers of this har-

APPENDIX. 199

poon are so formed, (being as already stated, six inches in width,) as to make a wide wound in piercing the fish: it is quite obvious, that, exactly in proportion to the width of the passage, which the weapon cuts in forcing its way into the fish, will be the space left open for its retraction; by the facility thus given for the instrument to withdraw itself, many stricken fish have been lost. I was assured by several masters of Greenland ships, that this accident had occurred to them, and that it will generally take place, when the harpoon is struck into a fish whose back is depressed, or when the flesh is in a relaxed state. When, therefore, the fish were less shy, and could be approached near enough, the hand harpoon frequently failed in its object; and since the fish have grown more difficult of approach, its defect has of course become of greater importance.

To obviate at once, the disadvantages arising from want of force in the hand harpoon, and from the great distance at which the whales often kept their pursuers, a harpoon to be discharged from a gun was suggested, patronised, and the inventor justly rewarded. Such a mode, it was confidently thought, would overcome both difficulties; but this confidence has unfortunately been disappointed.

I am acquainted with the form of three harpoons that have been used from guns, they are correctly represented in the subjoined figures.

1st. A gun harpoon, the shank of which is a solid bar of iron, continued from a cylindrical butt, the size of the caliber of the piece; the rope is secured to a ring that slides on the shank.

2d. A gun harpoon, with the rope secured to it by a ring, that slides on one of the circular rods, forming the shank.

3d. A gun harpoon, with a bow line affixed to a collar.

It is plain, from these representations, that the objections to the shape of the hand harpoon, if well founded, apply equally to all three. But there are many other objections; as it is not possible for any of these weapons to go in a direct line to the object, no precise aim can be taken with the gun; nor will a gun that is to be fired from a swivel at the shoulder, admit, (because of the recoil) of a sufficient charge of gunpowder, to propel a heavy instrument,—placed in the manner in which the harpoon now is, with the required rapidity to the required distance.

In addition to the above defects, the velocity of these harpoons receives considerable check in the resistance occasioned by the rope affixed to the sliding collar; the harpoon cannot be thrown directly point foremost, but will fly with some degree of curvature, which makes it consequently liable to take a bad position, and likewise to wound with the shank as well as the point, thereby making a wide cut, through which it is drawn without any considerable strain. It is also to be noted, that, in fastening the line to the harpoon, there is no mediate connexion between the iron and the rope; when the rope does not immediately join the harpoon, the danger of some part, particularly the ring breaking by the impetus of the discharge is always very great. Before I could succeed in my plan of gaining communication with vessels wrecked on a lee shore by a shot with a line attached to it, I failed in every instance, until I had discovered some material to connect the rope to the ball, that would withstand the shock of the discharge. I therefore speak on this point with the certainty of experience.

The following representation gives the gun, loaded with the harpoon, as on the point of being discharged.

It is evident, that so much of an instrument like the harpoon of considerable weight*, left protruding from the muzzle of the gun, must confine the point blank range to a very few yards indeed: the parabola, or curve, must take place almost at the very moment of discharge. To counteract this, the gun must, like a mortar, be fired at a great elevation: but the requisite geometrical means of ascertaining the due elevation cannot here be practised; and the aim must, consequently, always be uncertain. I have already noticed the very tardy flight of a body thus discharged, with a force inadequate to its weight; and, when to this want of velocity is added a circuitous direction, the fish may have dived from terror at the flash or re-

---

* Those which were sent me from Hull, and procured for the purpose of making experiments, exceeded seven pounds in weight, and were two feet and a half in length.

port, or, if it be moving with speed, may have passed, before the fall of the harpoon.

To shew that these objections are not merely theoretical, I add the observations of Captain Sanderson, of the ship Enterprise, of Lynn, a gentleman of great ability, and possessed of an experience of twenty years on the subject.

" In a calm, the fish are often numerous and playing about, but will not allow themselves to be approached near enough to be struck by the hand; therefore, if a *lock that will not miss fire and a gun to carry a harpoon that will not draw, and will go point blank at thirty yards, can be constructed*, the invention would be an invaluable acquisition, as hundreds of fish would then certainly be taken which cannot now be approached. These qualities in a gun-harpoon would do away *every obstacle* to the complete success of the Whale-Fishery."

I am not without confidence, that I have attained that which Captain Sanderson points out as all that is necessary to ensure certain success in this important branch of commerce. I trust that I have invented a substitute for the gun-harpoon, *the point blank of which will be upwards of thirty yards*, and the construction of which, by a mechanical combination to produce strength, will *effectually prevent its retraction;* while it shall be sure to fly with its *point directly foremost*, and make a *wound not so large as its own breadth*, and be prevented taking a *bad position* in the fish. *This will be discharged from a gun, not liable to miss fire*, even in the most boisterous weather, when properly attended to. I have reason to believe too, that the substitute which I propose for the harpoon will be discharged with a *force* that will enable it to pierce the *intestines* of the fish, (the sensitive seat of its energy and vitality) thereby depriving it of the power of making those violent exertions which cause great difficulty in securing it, and often endanger the lives of those engaged in the pursuit.

CERTIFICATE.

We, the under-signed, Merchants, Ship-Owners, &c., residing at *Yarmouth*, have this day, at the request of *Captain Manby*, attended an experiment of his New-invented *gun-harpoon*, and do Certify, that the Harpoon is discharged from the Gun, and flies with a true position, point blank, upwards of Thirty Yards, through an Inch Board, and, from the construction of the Lock, it is not probable the Gun will miss fire—and we do further certify, that it appears to us, from the formation of the Harpoon, it is not likely to draw after it has struck the Fish.

     W. PALGRAVE, JUN., *Collr. Customs.*
     SAMUEL PAGET.
     TIMOTHY STEWARD.
     AMBROSE PALMER.
     DAWSON TURNER.

YARMOUTH, 9th *Feb.* 1820.

The following figure represents the harpoon, with which the experiment here certified was made. It was two inches in diameter, seven inches in length, and weighed 3lb. 1oz. The rope was fastened to it by stout strips of raw ox-hide, capable of enduring the powerful inflammation of the powder without injury, and plaited very closely. The harpoon had a wooden cap at that end which was first introduced into the gun.

The arms or withers of this harpoon were let into a mortice made to receive them, sufficiently deep to admit of their going freely into the caliber of the piece; the withers were of iron, highly tempered to give them the most resisting strength.

It is here necessary to observe, that, in the construction of the harpoons in use, the greatest attention is paid to making those instruments of the softest and most pliable iron, to prevent the liability of that important part, the *shank*, breaking, and to admit of its twisting, or bending readily; for which purpose, the harpoons undergo the process of softening, by very gradual or protracted cooling; a process, which, however advantageous to render the shank yielding, must no doubt be injurious to the withers, to which cause, it is probable that the bending or upsetting of the withers of many is to be ascribed.

This is completely obviated in the harpoon shown above, for the withers being detached, admit of the most powerful hardening, and the combined lockings, when united, supply it with all the strength that can be required.

The harpoon is given below with its conical end, and screw point, prepared to enter into the wooden cap, which is hollowed out to receive that extremity.

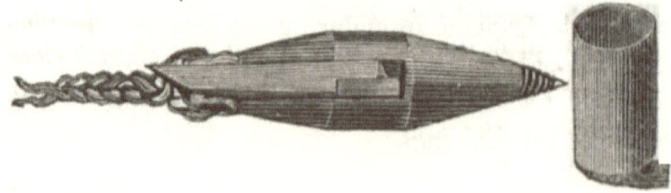

The worm of the screw entering into the wood, firmly secures it to the harpoon, and forms one compact body. The design of the cap is to remove the loss of that power that would otherwise be caused, by leaving a space between the gunpowder and the point of the instrument. It also keeps the harpoon centrifugally in the gun to receive the

APPENDIX. 205

greatest impulse, and to destroy that friction which so much diminishes the force and accuracy of flight of the harpoons now in use. On the discharge, the harpoon is disengaged from the wooden cap, by the splitting of the latter.

To cause the withers to extend beyond the orifice made by the harpoon, and to ensure their catching, springs were added as here represented.

Neither the lock of the gun mentioned in the certificate, nor the gun itself, possessed any originality, (and only a simple means was used to prevent the gun from going off by accident, by a cover over the hammer); it exploded the charge by percussion, giving a *powerful stroke* upon *well primed and dried* fulminating composition, in copper caps, which effectually defied the elements to prevent the use of the instrument: much attention is requisite in employing this composition, but when that attention is scrupulously paid, it will never fail; in confirmation, I have exploded more than a hundred primings in succession without one having missed.

The gun used in the experiments was two inches in diameter, in the bore, and fourteen inches in length, having at the bottom a chamber and antechamber for the more immediate manner of exploding the charge, and producing the greatest velocity.

The preceding remarks on the failure of late years, in taking whales with the certificate I did myself the honour of sending to Captain Scoresby, as a gentleman of great experience on the subject, and, in return, had the pleasure of receiving from him an encouragement of the hopes I had conceived of my apparatus. The following is an extract from his letter to me:—

"The certificate subjoined to your remarks is most satisfactory; and if the line used in your experiment be equal to those usually employed, it evinces a degree of power in the gun, of which the harpoon at present in use is totally incapable. The best harpoon guns, with which I am acquainted, are capable of projecting a harpoon in a point blank direction only about twenty yards; and then the harpoon usually penetrates obliquely, and occasions such a large wound as renders the instrument liable to draw."

This opinion of Captain Scoresby renders it incumbent upon me to declare, that the experiments which I have made with my harpoon assure me that, with a gun of less weight than any now in use and much shorter, *I can project my harpoon attached to a rope of the usual size, thirty yards in a point blank direction.*

The flight of the harpoon for that distance *is quite direct*; and the wound made by it can consequently be no greater in size than the girt of the weapon. This I have proved: the plank through which it was fired, contracting, as wood always does, after a sudden and violent perforation, presented a hole less in diameter than the instrument that made it.

I have to add (in allusion to the end of the extract from Captain Scoresby's letter) that, whatever other objections may be urged (though I hope and trust none can) against the harpoon which I have invented, it can never be alleged, that it will be liable to retraction through the wound which it shall have made in piercing the fish. From its construction, *I pronounce such an accident to be impossible.* If, then, there were no other benefit gained by my plan, this would, of itself, I venture to assert, be no slight improvement. It is well known frequently to happen, especially in what are called slack-backed fish, that the spasmodic convulsion and contraction, which attend the stroke of the harpoon, is instantly followed by a violent heaving and distention of the part, by which the wound is presented twice as wide as the barbs of the instrument which made it, and is therefore often cast back out of it. A great many fish have thus escaped, as I have already had occasion to observe. I trust, therefore, I shall not be thought presumptuous, when I say, that, if I obviated this risque alone, (which I am confident I have done,) my harpoon would merit a preference to all hitherto in use.

To the letter which Captain Scoresby so politely sent me, he added, in the most handsome manner, the gratifying present of his account of the Arctic Regions, with a history and description of the Northern Whale Fishery; a work, to which the deep science and long experience of the author have combined to give the utmost value; and I gladly avail myself of it, as the highest authority both to corroborate what I had before stated on the subject, and to give weight to some further observations.

Captain Scoresby remarks, that "there is a great difficulty, in calm clear weather, to approach a whale near enough to be struck by the hand."

"In calm clear weather, the whales take the alarm, when boats approach within fifteen or twenty yards of them."

"Much address is requisite to get near enough for the harpooner to strike a fish by the hand; and, if it indicates an intention of diving before the boat is near enough for that purpose, the harpoon is thrown by the hand, which a skilful man would accomplish at a distance of eight to ten yards.

It must be concluded from these remarks, that, in calm

weather, the capture of whales by the hand-harpoon is extremely uncertain; even if the animal allows a boat to approach within eight or ten yards before it dives, how very doubtful must be the effect of the harpoon, when darted by the hand at such a distance. When it is considered, how comparatively small the force of the strongest and most expert arm is; that the harpoon is necessarily an instrument of considerable weight, in order to give it strength; and that it is encumbered and retarded in its flight, by a train of thick rope; what reasonable assurance can there be, that it will pierce deep enough to retain its hold against the violent efforts which the fish makes to disengage itself?

When a whale is so effectually stricken, that the harpoons hold, the pursuers are obliged to use long lances, as often as, on its rising to breathe, they can approach near enough to pierce it, that, by loss of blood, or wounds in its *vitals*, they may deprive it of that tremendous power, which it might otherwise use to free itself from the line. Now, I have reason for the opinion, that the gun-harpoon, which I propose, will at once wound the fish *too deeply*, to permit it to exert that astonishing strength, which it so often employs successfully in effecting its escape and occasioning the loss of lines and harpoons without number, sometimes of the boat itself, and not unfrequently of the lives of the crew. The favourite resort of *Large Whales* for security, instinct has taught them to choose near the edges of extensive bodies of close *pack** or compact *patch*† ice,

---

* *Pack Ice* is an assemblage of large pieces of ice in such quantities, that the extent of the mass cannot be discerned. The fragments of pack ice, though generally near each other, do not touch.

† *Patch Ice* is composed of pieces overlapping or nearly joining

where it is often difficult, and in many instances impossible, to take them. Such situations afford refuge to the fish when alarmed or wounded, and enable them to flee beyond the reach of their pursuers; finding sufficient openings to allow them to respire, they can drag thither after them any quantity of line, which the fishers are obliged generally to cut, and thus to abandon the whale, lest the boat and crew should be drawn under the ice. To prevent such calamity to the crew, and, at the same time, not to forego all chance of securing the fish, when the boat's complement of lines are all run out, and no further supply is at hand, it is sometimes a practice with the fishers, on being drawn to the edge of the ice, to abandon the boat in the hope that it may serve as a buoy to recover the materials, and also the fish*; in preference to cutting the line; this risk, often resorted to, is by fishers termed, *" giving a whale the boat."*

Captain Scoresby in speaking of *pack* fishing, states, that instances have occurred of fish having been entangled during forty or fifty hours, and having escaped after all; and of ships having lost the greatest part of their stock of lines, several of their boats, and even, though happily less commonly, some individuals of their crews.

Captain Taylor, who formerly commanded the Duncombe, and who sailed with me in the Baffin, assured me, that in one voyage while he was master of that ship, he had lost *sixteen large fish* which he had struck, with his lines and harpoons, from their effecting their escape under such ice. And I myself saw the Trafalgar strike a fish which we afterwards heard was lost from a similar cause; now these losses I have no doubt might be materially remedied, and

each other, where the extent of the mass, though considerable, can be discerned.

* This plan was adopted by the Trafalgar, and we were afterwards so fortunate as to capture the fish, boat and lines.

the fish often secured, by the use of my proposed harpoon from a gun, or shells, if skilfully applied.

The inefficacy of the hand-harpoon is sufficiently evinced both by the complaints of those engaged in the fishery, and by the *great excitements* held out in the shape of remunerations by the *Society of Arts, Commerce, and Manufactures*, to those who invented gun-harpoons; and those who were most successful in the use of them.

Some of the gun-harpoons, already in use, though they have by no means performed what was desired, have, amongst many instances of failure, enabled those who used them to strike fish, which could not have been reached by the hand. The instances of failure have been in some cases attributable to the inadequacy of the instruments to their purpose; but more frequently to want of skill in those who had the direction of them. Between these two causes, they have fallen into total neglect.—Captain Scoresby writes thus on this subject:—

" The loss of many fish, from unskilful hands using the gun-harpoon, has thrown it into disuse."

In another part of his most excellent work, he says— " By some, the gun-harpoon is held in prejudiced aversion."

With regard to the first of these observations, I would remark, that the well-known inefficacy of the present gun-harpoon, in *many*, is very likely to have bred the distrust of it which exists in *all*, cases. It is the natural consequence of such a distrust to check that exertion, which is required for the attainment of skill in its management. Men will make no efforts, where success is impossible; and they will be proportionably inert, when it is improbable.

The *prejudice* of which Captain Scoresby speaks against the *gun-harpoon*, at present known, I regret to say, was admitted by all conversant in the concerns of the fishery, of whom I made inquiries; a circumstance, that excited no small degree of astonishment in my mind, from the *self-*

evident advantage of a harpoon propelled by the powerful influence of powder, over that projected from the hand. I have repeatedly asked, whether it was ever known that a whale had been *instantly* killed by the stroke of a hand harpoon? The answer has been invariably, No. But when I have demanded, whether such a case had ever occurred with the gun harpoon, the reply has been, That such instances were frequent; and some of my informants were the very persons who had inflicted the deadly wound. This clearly proves the want of sufficient projectile power in the hand, to reach the viscera of the fish; and is very satisfactory on the decided advantage of the weapon propelled from a gun. This important conclusion is confirmed by Captain Scoresby; he says "A hundred superficial wounds received by harpoons, could not have the effect of a single lance penetrating the vitals."

From these circumstances, I was naturally induced to suspect that the minds of those concerned in the use of the gun must be disposed to resist every attempt at improvement, with an obstinate adherence to old customs, or must be swayed by those hostile impressions congenial to hearts, where self-interest is the ruling passion. Reflections warned me to be circumspect into whose hands my instruments should be placed for trial, least some mismanagement might annihilate its intention; I well knew that many an useful invention has been thrown into discredit, from an unfavourable opinion being formed of its utility, by those deputed to apply it, and that after the failure of one experiment, it is difficult, if not impossible, to produce conviction by the success of future operations. To remove this apprehension, and to establish the confidence which I had formed of the utility of my invention, could, it appeared, be effected only by personal superintendence. I, therefore, at once determined manfully to encounter every inconvenience, by a voyage to Greenland, to direct its operations; I could thus obtain opinions, upon the spot, of the instrument from masters of ships, best qualified to judge of their merits; I could observe with scrutinizing attention, how the business was carried on, and whether the implements were adequate to their purpose; and by attentive observation, I could also investigate the cause of the prejudice against the permanent introduction of the gun; and by learning whether any part of the system was injurious to the interest of those most concerned in the fishery, might be enabled faithfully to report the fact to them.

To Captain Scoresby, Commander of the Baffin belonging to Liverpool, from his distinguished experience in the Northern Whale Fishery, and profound scientific knowledge, I applied for a passage in his ship, and he most readily acceded to my views, by an invitation to accompany him; and I lost no time in perfecting such improvements in the gun and hand harpoon, as appeared requisite, for the more effectual taking of whales; as well as in the shells and carcasses intended to lessen the torture that often attends the present method of killing fish, I considered it due to humanity, that their sufferings should be terminated as speedily as possible*; and it was likewise a primary object to determine, whether the shells were sufficiently effective to remove the hazard, often attendant on the service of lancing vicious or dangerous fish.

On getting to sea, as soon as leisure permitted, my inventions were submitted to Captain Scoresby, and their several intentions explained in the presence of the har-

---

* I have had communicated to me instances of a fish, having 10, 12, and more harpoons in it, and of every stratagem being used to irritate the wounds, in order to produce pain, and facilitate its death; yet the fish has endured the agony of these goadings for many hours.

pooners of the ship; I distinctly declared that the object of my voyage to Greenland was solely a desire to benefit the fishery; and all I required was a *fair trial* of my several instruments to determine *their merits.*

For this purpose, Captain Scoresby appointed to the boat intended for the service, a harpooner who was making his first voyage in that capacity, as one best calculated for a new practice in the fishery; but most unfortunately he was soon after violently attacked by illness. From conversation with the other harpooners, my suspicions were established of an inveterate jealousy existing against any novel practice, and particularly with regard to the application of a gun-harpoon; I was indeed assured in confidence by one of the crew, on whose veracity I could rely, that the following declaration had been made, " *that if the gun succeeded it might lead to its more general use, and that every man then, who could point a gun, could act as a harpooner;*" and further that the minds of most of the crew had been influenced to express a wish for its failure. After this, water was actually poured into one of my guns by some miscreant; no doubt with the object of defeating the success of the invention.

From these circumstances, I considered the harpooner not sufficiently unprejudiced to sit in judgment on its utility, and determined to await until the man was restored to health, who had been appointed to the service of the gun-boat; and in the mean time I resolved to make myself master of the process of fishing, by accompanying expeditions, and minutely observing every transaction in taking fish by the hand-harpoon.

The following is an extract from the journal of Captain Scoresby, describing my implements, &c., with which he favoured me.

Extract, May 29, 1821, respecting Captain Manby's new method of taking whales.

" Hitherto, owing to the indisposition of the harpooner appointed to take charge of Captain Manby's apparatus for killing whales, no opportunity has occurred of applying any of the instruments to practice; it is time, however, that I should give some description of the apparatus, for the trial of which, Captain Manby, at an advanced period of life, (fifty-six) has been induced to forego the enjoyments of a peaceful and happy home, to encounter the rigour and privation of a Greenland voyage; and this, not from motives of personal emolument, but, with his usual philanthropy, with the view of contributing to the success of a branch of trade, the highest in the scale of national importance, and of diminishing, as far as may be, the dangers of the occupation; whatever, therefore, may be the fate of his invention, he is entitled to the full praise of having employed his property and his ingenuity for the promotion of a public benefit, and deserves well of his country."

" Captain Manby has invented three or four different pieces of apparatus, viz.:

" 1st. A hand-harpoon constructed with jointed spring barbs, intended to prevent the liability of retraction.

" 2d. A gun-harpoon for the same purpose, calculated, he conceives, to afford greater precision in direction, to take effect at greater distances, and to be more capable of retention when it penetrates, than the gun-harpoon at present in use.

" 3d. A small gun with shells and carcasses for killing whales without the use of the lance.

APPENDIX. 215

"Fig. 1. Hand-harpoons with barbs have already been tried; but the whole have failed in consequence of the weakness of the joint*; they were of this form:

Fig. 1.

But Captain Manby's joint of the withers is extremely ingenious, and promises the greatest possible security of which such a contrivance is susceptible.

Fig. 2.

"Fig. 2, is a representation of the harpoon with the withers when tied together †.

Fig. 3.

"In Figure 3 they are expanded.

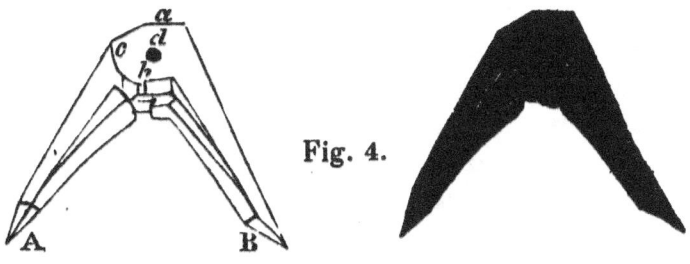

Fig. 4.

"Figure 4 shows the barbs or withers detached.

* In this harpoon, the reliance for security depends entirely on the pins.

† On this principle the reliance for security does *not* depend

Fig 5.

"The upper part of the mortice in the shank, which receives the hinge of the wither, is here removed to show the lockings from which the joint derives its strength. Thus in figure 4, the wither A when expanded, locks against the fore part of the mortice, and at b against the septum in the back of the mortice, and at c against the other wither B; while in addition to these lockings, the withers are kept in their place by a strong screw pin d: the upper surface of the wither B, and the lower surface of A are filed down at the joint part, to exactly one half of their original thickness, so as together to coincide to the thickness of the withers externally, and to form a single equal plane when closed. In figure 5 are two springs by which the withers are forced asunder; in striking this harpoon the withers collapse, and only make an opening three inches wide, but the moment a strain is applied to withdraw it, the points become inserted in the blubber of the whale, and by means of the inclined planes at A and B, (Fig. 4) together with the efforts of the springs, they are separated, as the instrument withdraws, to the width of 7 inches. In this harpoon, I conceive, that the joint, which in all other harpoons of the kind has been the failing part, is as perfect, and as strong as could be wished. Comprising less breadth than the common harpoon, it must be more easily thrust into the fish; and making an opening only one half the size of the expanded withers, it will have less chance of retracting. The

upon the pins; for were the pins to be displaced, the harpoon, once fixed in the fish, would retain its hold by the withers being morticed.

APPENDIX. 217

shank, however, is too short and too thick, of which defects, Captain Manby is now aware; nor do they, indeed, in the least degree lessen the merit of the principle. I am also in some doubt whether the withers towards the point be not too weak: this likewise has no reference to the principle: in old fish, the fibre of whose blubber is very tenacious, I believe that Captain Manby's harpoon, if sufficiently strong in manufacture, could not be withdrawn by the strength of a whale line, though such a line is capable of sustaining a weight of more than two tons, perhaps 2¾ tons, when new, of the best hemp, and manufacture 2¼ inches thick. But in young fish, there is little doubt but that *this* or any harpoon might be drawn through the whole thickness of fat, though no cut whatever had been made for its insertion, in consequence of the want of strength of the tendinous fibre of the blubber.

" Captain Manby's gun-harpoon is on an *entirely* new principle, both in its construction, and in the manner of firing it. It is represented by figure 6.

Fig. 6.

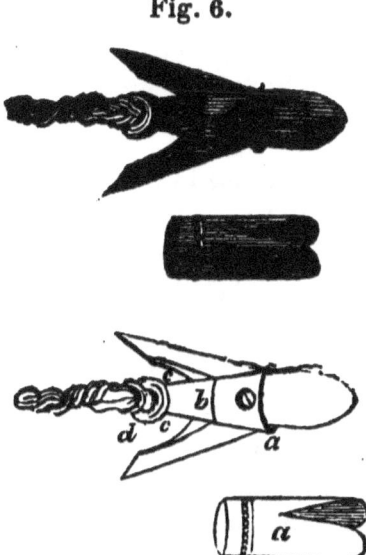

"This harpoon which is made of brass or iron, or steel, is morticed from a to b for the reception of the withers, in the same manner as the hand-harpoon, and the lockings of the withers are on the same principle; but the springs for opening the withers are attached to the wither *(c,)* instead of to the mark of the harpoon, as in the former instruments; from the point *b* to *a* the instrument is sharp, but the outer edges of the withers are blunt and square, as they occupy only the same breadth as the cutting part of the mouth. To the opening *d* is attached a rope platted of raw hide, or wire to prevent injury in the firing, and of about a yard in length; with this is connected the usual foreganger and line. The novelty of application in this harpoon consists in its being fired with the part *d* foremost: in effecting the discharge, a cylindrical cap *a*, of wood, three inches long and two inches in diameter is fitted on the point of the harpoon, the cap being scooped out for its reception. The harpoon is then thrust, point first, in the state represented by figure 7, into the gun.

Fig. 7.

"The re-action of the line in the heel of the harpoon inverts it soon after it leaves the muzzle of the gun, and keeps its point foremost in the flight. The harpoon, which is cylindrical at the middle, and nine inches long by two inches in diameter, weighs about 5½lbs. Captain Manby thinks it capable of carrying a line direct, or point blank, twenty-five yards, while, in the experiments he made, the common gun-harpoon only went nine yards *point blank* before it struck the ground with the point, and twenty-nine yards, when elevated 15° or 17°. The advantages of this harpoon, therefore appear, to be, its point blank direction, the small orifice which it makes, and its power of retention whenever it penetrates.

"Capt. Manby's idea of affording a method of destroying whales by shells and carcasses thrown from a gun, seems to be quite original, and promises, if the shells have power of penetration sufficient, to be an admirable auxiliary means of capturing whales: for attacking "*wicked fish*," fish at the edge of packs, finners, razor backs, &c., these destructive implements might be of uncommon service. There can be little doubt that a shell, exploding among the viscera of a fish, would produce instant paralysis; this being the case, fish might then be attacked without hazard at packs, or in a sea, or amid bay ice; when, in the ordinary way, they could not be struck without the most imminent risk of the loss of lines and materials, while the chance of succeeding in the capture is small. Such are Captain Manby's inventions: they are the result of a persevering, thinking and comprehensive mind: a mind devoted to philanthropic objects, and to the public good."

The shells were of cast-iron in an oblong form, $1\frac{1}{2}$ diameter in length; the fuzes were of brass having a strong thread, to screw them securely into the mouth of the shell, in which was cut a female screw to receive it: the fuze was driven with powder (of the strongest quality) mealed, and the length graduated to burn as nearly one second as possible, and the head was pierced with four holes for pieces of quick match drawn through them, to ensure the fuze igniting from the flash of the gun.

The carcasses were of similar form to the shells, with a much larger mouth (where was also cut a female screw,) to receive pieces of an unextinguishable composition which generated a gas destructive to vitality; the mouth was closed by a screw to prevent the pieces of composition being blown out: and in the sides were holes (filled up with mealed powder moistened with spirits of wine, and primed with pieces of quick match,) to permit the fury of the fire issuing through them to produce instantaneous destruction.

The harpooner appointed to the service of the gun-boat getting better, and on the 7th of June several whales having been seen, all the boats were despatched in readiness for pursuit, and ordered to different stations near the edge of the ice to await the re-appearance of the fish: the particulars of this expedition have already been stated in the journal. Here I had the mortification of seeing five or six ineffectual heaves of hand-harpoons at fish, which would certainly have been taken by a gun; and fortune now conspired to disappoint me, for not a single fish afterwards approached us nearer than 2 or 300 yards, though every effort was made both by lying in wait, and in chase. The harpooner, having evidently received the contagion of prejudice, his conduct so displeased me, that in the anger of my feelings, I determined to take no further part in the exertion; and, strange to say, after the following day, there never was a chance of taking a fish, although we sailed through many hundred leagues of apparently as fine fishing water and as favourable ice as ever were seen.

The opinion formed of the implements* by the many experienced persons to whom they were exhibited when in Greenland. was without exception, that of general approbation; and I shall here give a copy of a letter from a Greenland Commander, whose experience in the gun-harpoon has particularly distinguished him, and whose opi-

---

* Should they be acceptable to the public, and worthy the adoption of those concerned in the whale-fishery, I respectfully beg leave to recommend Mr. Beckwith, Gun Manufacturer, Skinner-street, London, and Mr. Samuel Moore, Smith, Yarmouth, as persons eminently qualified to give them the highest degree of perfection and utility.

nion from a service of twenty-two years in the fishery, is entitled to much respect.

Deptford, Dec. 18, 1821.

" Sir,

" Having been eleven years master of Greenland Ships, and received a premium from the Honourable Society of Arts and Sciences, for shooting whales, I was induced to come on board the Baffin, when in sight of the west land of Greenland, to be introduced to you, for the purpose of seeing your improved implements for the fishery, which have my *fullest approbation*, and are, as I stated to you when we met in Greenland, better adapted to the purposes intended, than those already known.

" When your hand-harpoon, were once well fast in a fish, it would from its construction, I should conceive, be impossible to draw it; nor could the withers upset, from the combined strength given to them.

" The harpoons to be discharged from a gun, I should also imagine must fly in a true and point blank direction, and having the same mechanical principle, as the hand-harpoon must possess the like important advantages.

" The shell for firing into whales from a gun, is the best invention with which I am acquainted, for the aid of the fishery, for a shell bursting in the body of a fish, will, no doubt, instantly destroy its power; and when used in attacking wicked fish, will be *invaluable*.

" You may, Sir, remember seeing the corpse of the boat-steerer of the Vigilant, who was killed while lancing a fish, not far from us; his life, as well as that of many others I have known, would have certainly been saved by such means.

I am, Sir,
Your most obedient humble servant,
ROBERT HAYS,
Late Master of the Ship Experiment."

" To Captain Manby."

In consequence of Captain Scoresby's expression in the extract from his journal, of " his apprehension, whether the shells possessed sufficient power of penetration for the purpose designed," although, satisfied in my own mind, that they did, I thought the question deserving both of reflection and experiment, as emanating from one of so much experience and discernment; I was, therefore, induced to give them a spear point, and to adapt them to the guns now in use; the result from experiment was a penetration nearly one half deeper, than that of the oblong shells through the same resisting medium.

These shells were made $2\frac{1}{2}$ diameters in length, and from the point nearly one diameter more; they were of solid metal, not only to give strength, but to preserve direction, in their flight: as the fuze was now necessarily next the charge of the gun, great precaution was requisite to prevent accident; this has been effectually done by the head of the fuze being let into a stout wad of cork, with a small perforation, to admit strands of quick match crossing, and to pass through the head of the fuze in the centre. On submitting this alteration in the construction of the shells to Captain Scoresby, the following is an extract from his reply:

" I ventured to differ in opinion with you, as to the power of penetration of the shells and carcasses, which, being oblong in their form, would probably fly in the direction of their shortest axis. You now inform me that you have been adapting a shell to the present harpoon-gun, with a spear point, that will, if required, go through a fish. Penetration was all the former shell wanted; for there can be no doubt, but a shell or carcass introduced into the body of a whale, must be the most efficient means of facilitating the capture ever devised. It would be fully as effectual as the rocket, when it takes effect in the best possible way, and incalculably more manageable."

I have now concluded my remarks on, and description of, the implements designed to improve the whale-fishery; from a sense of duty, and in justice to myself, I have detailed the circumstances that occurred on my Greenland voyage, and also my opinion of the causes which have hitherto defeated the object so long and liberally patronised by the Society of Arts, Commerce, and Manufactures, for the general introduction of the gun-harpoon; I have also had in view to lay before those most immediately concerned in the fishery, some of the causes which have in numerous instances entailed a want of success on their speculation; and I shall close the subject with a few observations which I respectfully submit to their consideration, as alterations necessary in the arrangement of Greenland ships.

The harpooners do not support a distinction of rank, so necessary in all services, to subordination and good order; the consequence is, that familiarity creates an influence which should not exist, and the crew become ready instruments in any line of conduct which the harpooners may capriciously take. This I saw confirmed in the Baffin, as every discontent and dissatisfaction that occurred during the voyage, originated with some of that class: I would recommend that they should mess apart, that their births should be detached, and themselves separated from the crew when not on duty; and that when on duty, they should be taught to conduct themselves as officers; they should be made to know that it is not absolutely necessary for every harpooner in the ship to have had the service of his life confined to that of the navigation of ice; but that a part of the number may be composed of steady, active seamen, who have served long in the navy, and particularly those used to the service of guns, who, if they were instructed in the management of a whale line, would, from their professional habits in pointing a gun with accuracy, although they should never have been in Greenland before, prove themselves superior harpooners to many, who have spent all their lives in the service. These considerations, I am inclined to hope, would excite a partiality to the use of the gun-harpoon. A proper sense of duty and zeal for their employers' benefit might be excited in the minds of the harpooners, by inducing them plainly to see, that as many fish may be taken by a gun-harpoon, as by the hand harpoon; and by making them, at the same time, understand, that their emoluments will not be diminished, it would be reasonable to suppose, that it could not then but be indifferent to them which they employed. Go farther, and convince them, that *more* fish must be taken by a gun than by a hand-harpoon; and assure them, that their perquisites shall be increased in exact proportion; and can it be supposed, that they will hesitate to give a preference to the former?

But should these endeavours and encouragements fail in making their owners' benefit their primary consideration; let the masters be directed by the owners, to despatch a boat carrying a gun as one of those *first* sent in pursuit on a fish being seen, and to hold out a further gratuity for a fish taken by the gun, beyond the sum at present allowed to the first fast boat: and, in order to produce additional incitement to the crew, and *attention* in the manager of the gun towards striking the fish in a *vital* place, so as to cause *instant death;* let it be determined that one whale being taken *without the aid* of a second harpoon, the harpooner shall receive two guineas, and the boats' crew one guinea each, in lieu of the usual bounty of half a guinea each to the crew of the first fast boat.

If the gun should be brought into general use, and scientifically applied, which I have no hesitation in saying, would, in many cases, remove the causes of failure; I should suggest the propriety of men, who are anxious to be employed as harpooners exercising themselves at a mark, as it must be evident that those most skilled as marksmen, would bring with them a high recommendation in their favour; and if premiums were given by the owners to be shot for as prizes, at some of the greatest ports, where Greenland ships are fitted out, it might cause considerable emulation, and encourage the use of the gun. This might be done in the long interval between return from the fishery, and departure again. A very little practice would convince those who witnessed it of what may be effected; and encourage them to render themselves expert in the use of an instrument, which they would see must succeed, if well directed.

I cannot conclude these remarks without again expressing the hope, that I shall not be censured for the confidence with which I have spoken of the aptitude of my harpoon for its purpose. I ground this confidence not upon mere theory. It rests upon my own experiments and observations, attested by the highly respectable gentlemen, whose signatures are annexed to the certificate which I have laid before my readers; and upon the opinions of the many experienced persons to whom my inventions have been submitted. Thus supported, I trust, I shall not only escape the charge of vanity, but the imputation of being too sanguine in my expectations of encouragement to a plan, that offers a means of promoting the success of one of the most lucrative branches of commerce known to the country.

FINIS.

www.ingramcontent.com/pod-product-compliance
Lightning Source LLC
Chambersburg PA
CBHW020114010526
44115CB00008B/819